Bless Us, O Lord

"Sitting at the table to share a meal as a family is a true expression of being the domestic church. At the table we eat, talk, learn, argue, laugh, and cry together. At the table, we share the joy of being with relatives and friends as God's blessings. Robert Hamma invites us in this fabulous book to start this intimate moment as a domestic church and community in prayer. *Bless Us, O Lord* is a superb collection of prayers that traveled to us through history, born in different communities and circumstances and offered by a great diversity of women and men who saw God in all things. These prayers are summons to pray and eat together, knowing that we are part of a larger whole and that God always journeys with us."

Hosffman Ospino
Associate Professor of Theology and Religious Education
Boston College School of Theology and Ministry

"I love this practical prayer book for families. Parents know that dinnertime is one of the few moments throughout the day when a family can sit down, slow down, and enjoy each other's company. Catholic parents know that it is also one of the best times of day to pray with our kids. Robert Hamma has put together a creative collection of prayers to use as any family's dinnertime devotional. Hamma has a heart for the poor and the marginalized, and the prayers he offers in *Bless Us, O Lord* invite us to share in that sentiment. This book will help families grow closer to God, closer to each other, and closer to the many people who go without food each day."

Jared Dees
Founder of The Religion Teacher website
Author of *Christ in the Classroom*

"In today's busy world, the thought of praying together as a family may feel like a challenge. Thankfully, Robert Hamma's wonderful resource *Bless Us, O Lord* offers a simple invitation to gather as a family around the table and to lift our voices in prayer. Hamma's simple yet insightful words provide gentle structure and context for the moments and celebrations that fill our hearts and homes. Share them with your loved ones and witness how your lives are blessed and encouraged!"

Lisa M. Hendey
Founder of CatholicMom.com

"Parents are often looking for ways to teach their children the rudiments of Catholic faith. Such education tends to occur in informal moments such as prayer before meals rather than through official catechetical curricula. In *Bless Us, O Lord,* parents will find a resource that will assist them in their work of teaching their children to pray. Eating together is integral to life within the domestic Church, not just because it's a time to catch up with one another but also because it's an occasion to develop the disposition of gratitude. Through these prayers before meals for nearly every occasion a family might experience, Robert Hamma has given Christian families a resource for developing a posture of gratitude in everyday life. The prayers connect as much to the daily events of family life as they do to the liturgical year of the Church. This book of prayers will be a gift to every family."

Timothy P. O'Malley
Director of Education
The McGrath Institute for Church Life
University of Notre Dame

"*Bless Us, O Lord* is simply beautiful. Each family knows the difficulties associated with family prayer—giggling, wiggling, crying, pinching. It's the blessed chaos of the home, which as parents we try at least to calm for prayer if only for a moment. Often it's at the mealtime table that prayer is the hardest, which is why Robert Hamma's book is so wonderful and so welcome. This book is special first for its clarity and breadth. Prayers involving the whole of life—saints, seasons, special occasions, and even secular heroes such as Helen Keller and Anne Frank—help families capture the world for prayer, teaching us to gather up in prayer all things children (and even parents) learn and celebrate throughout life. But what is even more profound is that if families use this book well they will in time bring two important tables closer together—the table of the Eucharist and the family table—in one organic rhythm of life.

Rev. Joshua J. Whitfield
Pastor
St. Rita Catholic Community
Dallas, Texas

Bless Us, O Lord

A Family Treasury of Mealtime Prayers

Written and Compiled by

Robert M. Hamma

Ave Maria Press AVE Notre Dame, Indiana

Founded in 1865, Ave Maria Press is a ministry of the United States Province of Holy Cross.

www.avemariapress.com

Paperback: ISBN-13 978-1-59471-981-3

E-book: ISBN-13 978-1-59471-982-0

Cover image © gettyimages.com.

Cover and text design by Katherine Robinson.

Printed and bound in the United States of America.

Library of Congress Cataloging-in-Publication Data

Names: Hamma, Robert M., author.
Title: Bless us, O Lord : a family treasury of mealtime prayers / Robert M. Hamma.
Description: Notre Dame, Indiana : Ave Maria Press, 2020. | Summary: "Complete with original and traditional blessings, this open-and-go resource offers parents and caregivers the perfect words for every occasion-from observing saint feast days and liturgical seasons to celebrating a child's birthday or first day of school to remembering the life of a loved one. Readers will find fresh ideas and tools for living the liturgy"-- Provided by publisher.
Identifiers: LCCN 2020013320 (print) | LCCN 2020013321 (ebook) | ISBN 9781594719813 (paperback) | ISBN 9781594719820 (ebook)
Subjects: LCSH: Prayers.
Classification: LCC BV245 .H26 2020 (print) | LCC BV245 (ebook) | DDC 242--dc23
LC record available at https://lccn.loc.gov/2020013320
LC ebook record available at https://lccn.loc.gov/2020013321

For Theodore and Charles,

and for the grandchildren still to come,

may this book be your companion

as you grow!

Contents

Acknowledgments

There are so many people who have helped bring this book to publication. I would like to thank the many colleagues and friends at Ave Maria Press: the publisher Tom Grady and the entire publishing team who have created it with such care, and my editor, Kristi McDonald, who personally tested the prayers and stories with her own young family.

My friends in the Diocese of Brooklyn, Msgr. Fernando Ferrarese and Msgr. Sean Ogle, were a great help in obtaining Korean and Vietnamese translations. Thanks to Fr. Alex Sangbin Lee for the translation of the feast of Sts. Andrew Kim Taegon and Companions and to Fr. Jun Hee Lee for the translation of St Andrew Dung-Lac and Companions. Thanks also to Joan Mader, C.S.C., for checking the Spanish texts.

And thanks to my family, who were the inspiration for this book: my loving wife, Kathy Schneider, who is my daily prayer companion at table, and my now-adult children and their spouses: Peter and Amy, Christine and Jon, and Sarah and Jake. You are the joy of our hearts! And to our grandchildren, Teddy and Charlie, who give us so much joy and hope for the future!

Introduction

Praying together as a family before meals has been one of the greatest joys of being a parent. As we gather around each meal—whether made from scratch, microwaved from a box, or fetched from the supermarket—I am reminded that everything we have is a gift from God. This daily ritual has become a natural way for me as a parent to pray with my children and to model for them that I am a person who prays. Practically speaking, it has become our formal way to begin a meal together: at the table, with everyone present, the television off, and all devices set aside.

Naturally, everyone does not always participate wholeheartedly or cheerfully, and the meal that follows the prayer often has a fair share of raucous behavior, teasing, spilt milk, and frayed tempers. Nevertheless, that moment of calm at the beginning sets a tone of gratitude and calls us to think, albeit briefly, about the person whose hand is in ours as we pray.

I still recall an experience that occurred years ago. We were at a friend's house for dinner. While I sat waiting for a signal to begin the meal, our two-year-old daughter reached out and took the hand of the child next to her. When the child asked why she had done that, we explained it was our family custom to say grace. Then we all joined hands and prayed the familiar words, "God is great, God is good, let us thank God for this food." As smiles of embarrassment broke out around the table, I marveled at the way my daughter, who was not yet old enough to know the words of the prayer, had helped us let down our guard and open up to God's presence in one another.

Jesus' presence at meals seems to have had the same effect. All the gospels record how frequently Jesus took the opportunity of a shared meal to teach, challenge, comfort, and forgive. But even more importantly, all of Jesus' meals were opportunities for his companions to open their hearts to him, to recognize him as did the two disciples on the road to Emmaus when he broke bread with them.

This was true regardless of whom his dining companions were. Outcasts such as Zacchaeus the tax collector, powerful people such as Simon the Pharisee, or friends and disciples such as Martha and Mary, all experienced meals with Jesus that brought about important changes in their lives. I imagine that if we could ask people who actually knew Jesus about their most memorable moment with him, many would say, "It was that time when we were eating and he. . . ." Perhaps that is part of the reason why Jesus left us the sacrament of sharing bread and wine in the Eucharist as the best way to remember him, saying, "Do this in memory of me."

We can remember him not only at the eucharistic table of the altar but also at our family tables. While every one of our family meals won't have the same dramatic effect as the meals Jesus shared with people such as Zacchaeus or Martha, they will certainly make a difference over the long run. The regular practice of saying grace helps create an atmosphere where gratitude to God, respect for one another, and concern for those in need can grow. At the very least, prioritizing prayer as a family sends a message to our children and ourselves that God is at the center of our lives and family.

Grace before meals is also a practical way to acknowledge and celebrate special family occasions. Including in family prayer our birthdays, anniversaries, family visits, school plays, and big games helps children recognize that God is present in all of these moments. They are opportunities to thank God for the love and care our family has shown us as well as to celebrate the gifts and talents that God has given us. All of these occasions can be moments of grace. I have included prayers for these celebrations in the "Special Occasions" section of this book.

One of my family's favorite prayers in this book is the prayer for a child's birthday. When they were young, my children loved it when their siblings would name a good quality of theirs or point out certain things that they did for which they were grateful. As they grew into adults, they introduced this practice to their friends and loved ones. We still use it today, often modifying the prayer to use with our adult friends who are with us on their birthdays.

Of course, everyone likes to hear nice things about themselves, and that's a fine gift to give someone on their birthday. But these prayers are more than that. They are expressions of the fact that these good qualities are gifts of God. God has graced each of us with particular abilities and dispositions and called us to use those gifts for others. Naming these qualities and gifts acknowledges that God is their source and that we are grateful for the ways that our family members and friends have shared those gifts with us.

It's hard to pull off family meals these days with family members' different schedules. There are school, work, and activities calendars. The four seasons come and go with holidays and special events. And yet the Church's calendar is not just one more calendar to worry about. Many of the days that our society celebrates have Christian roots—for example, Halloween, Valentine's Day, or Mardi Gras. But more broadly, the Church year, or liturgical year, permeates all of our calendars. The seasons of Advent and Christmas, Lent and Easter, and Ordinary Time lead us to follow the life of Jesus throughout the year. Advent prayers remind us that preparation for Christmas is more than shopping and decorating. Observing the season of Christmas helps us remember the many rich aspects of the story of Christ's birth. Lenten prayers help us realize that Lent is more than giving up something; it's about doing something for others, especially the poor. Keeping Easter not just as a day but as a season provides an opportunity to explore the many dimensions of the Resurrection. Celebrating these seasons at our family meals helps us recognize Christ's presence and action in our lives. Whether it's the Advent wreath or a rice bowl, praying and observing seasonal traditions can form a lasting pattern of moving through the year that will accompany our children as they grow. You'll find these prayers included in "The Church Year" section.

The Church also celebrates the saints throughout the year. Remembering the saints reminds us that we are part of a Church that has a long history and has reached every corner of the world. Celebrating the saints takes us back to the beginning of the Church, to Jesus' followers and friends who left their ordinary lives behind to follow him. It places us with the martyrs in the Roman Colosseum and with the earliest monks in the desert. It takes us with the missionaries to explore unknown lands, from China and Japan to the Americas. It brings us to the universities, monasteries, and convents where theologians and mystics spent their lives in study and prayer. It also brings us to the poorest places in the world where saints selflessly gave their lives caring for the poor and the sick—the people whom society ignores and sometimes despises. What an exciting world to introduce to our children! These are the real superheroes who have changed and rescued our world.

In this book, I have tried to select those saints who would be most interesting to children: St. Thomas Aquinas was mocked by his classmates as a dumb ox; St. Damien of Molokai left a comfortable life in Belgium to work among lepers on the remote island of Molokai; and St. Isaac Jogues, who preached the Gospel to the Iroquois and Hurons, was tortured and killed by them. So many of these saints overcame incredible obstacles and hardships—some were orphans, slaves, or prisoners; some were poor and uneducated; and some lived selfish, pampered lives before they converted. Their stories are condensed here so as not to let the dinner get cold, but you may want to read more about them (there are lots of great websites) and tell their stories in full over dinner. You'll find these prayers included in "Holidays and Saints' Days through the Year" section.

A friend who encouraged me for years to publish this book recently told me that what she appreciated most about it was that the prayers so often call to mind the poor and the hungry. Gratitude for our blessings should make us aware of those who are not so fortunate. Praying for the hungry and the homeless, for refugees and victims of war, can lead us to look for ways to help them. As one of the Beatitudes reminds us, "Blessed are they who hunger and thirst for righteousness, for they will be satisfied" (Mt 5:6). As we nourish our families with food and drink, we should also nurture in them an awareness and desire to help those in need. Children are naturally God-centered, if properly guided. When exposed, but not coercively, to the devotional life of the Church, children spontaneously show their innate capacity for prayer and service. Speak often with your children about your faith, the saints, and the sacraments. Pray together whenever you think of it. These are the kinds of memories that children never forget.

In this book, I offer prayers in both English and a second language. The Church today, especially in the United States, is blessed to be composed of people from all over the world. In many parishes and dioceses, Mass is celebrated in a number of languages. To help families celebrate the traditions and saints of their native lands, I have included prayers in Spanish, Korean, and Vietnamese for a number of such days.

Some suggestions for using this book:

- Keep it handy, on or near the kitchen table.
- Have the children lead the prayers as they are able.
- Be alert to words or terms that younger children may not understand. Ask an older child to explain or do so yourself.
- Ask open-ended questions that arise from the particular day or the prayer. For example, on the Feast of Our Lady of Lourdes you might ask, "How do you think Bernadette felt when no one believed that she had seen Mary?" Or on the Feast of St. Catherine of Siena, "What do you think about Catherine giving away her family's food and clothing without asking?" Read the short biographies in advance and consider how you might make them a basis for family conversation.
- Dinner is not the only time you can use these prayers. A friend has used them at breakfast, the beginning of her homeschool day. They might also be used in a classroom as a grace before lunchtime.

In 1995, I was privileged to have Ave Maria Press, where I worked for twenty-five years, publish *Let's Say Grace*. This book has grown out of that one. Back then, our three children were eight, six, and three. The artist who designed the original book even included sketches of them. Time flies. Today they are all grown up. But there are new children in the family now—two young grandsons, Theodore and Charles. It is with them in mind, as well as the hope of more grandchildren one day, that I offer you this new book.

The Days of the Week

Sunday

Leader: This is the day the Lord has made.
All: Let us rejoice and be glad in it.

God, our Creator,
we thank you for this Sunday.
We thank you for our church,
for our home, and for the chance to rest today.
As we share this meal, help us to recognize
the presence of Jesus with us
and fill us with the joy of your Holy Spirit.
We ask this through Christ, our Lord.
Amen.

Leader: This is the day the Lord has made.
All: Let us rejoice and be glad in it.

Monday

We thank you, Lord, our God,
for this new week that we have begun today.
We thank you for our schools and for our work,
and for all our friends there.
Bless this food that we share
and give us the strength
to be patient and kind with one another.
Amen.

Tuesday

DEAR GOD,
your love is like a mother's gentle hands
and your care is like a father's watchful presence.
We thank you for always being there for us
and for giving us the gift of one another as a family.
During this meal, help us to listen to one another
and to appreciate each one's unique gifts.
We ask this in Jesus' name.
Amen.

Wednesday

GENEROUS GOD,
we give you thanks for this food
and for all the good things you have given us.
Help us to remember those who are hungry tonight.
Teach us how we can help all those who are in need.
We ask this through Christ, our Lord.
Amen.

Thursday

BLESSED ARE YOU, LORD, OUR GOD.
You made the land, the sea, the sun, and the rain.
You brought forth this food from nature's bounty to our table.
We thank you for the farmers who grew it
and for the many people who brought it
from the fields to the factories to the supermarkets.
And we thank you for (*name*) who cooked it for us.
Amen.

Friday

FATHER,
as we come to the end of another week of work
 and school,
we thank you for your friendship
and ask your forgiveness for our failings.
Help us to be more like your Son, Jesus,
who showed us his love on the Cross.
And make us grateful for all your gifts
and for this meal we now share.
Amen.

Saturday

LORD JESUS,
you are with us always
in our chores and in our play,
in what we do together
and when we are apart.
Help us to grow in love as a family
and to be a sign of your presence
to our friends and neighbors.
Thank you for this food and for this day.
Amen.

The Church Year

Advent

First Sunday

Leader: Come, Lord Jesus, set us free.
All: Come, Lord Jesus, come.

Light the first Advent candle.

THANK YOU, LORD, FOR THIS SEASON OF ADVENT
when we prepare for your coming.
Help us to keep our eyes open
to see you when you come to us.
Bless this food that reminds us of the banquet
we will all share with you one day in heaven.
Amen.

Leader: Come, Lord Jesus, set us free.
All: Come, Lord Jesus, come.

Weekdays of the First Week

Leader: Come, Lord Jesus, bless this food.
All: Come, Lord Jesus, come.

Light the first Advent candle.

LORD, AS WE BEGIN TO GET READY FOR CHRISTMAS,
help us to be grateful for all your gifts,
especially the gift of this meal we share together.
Amen.

Leader: Come, Lord Jesus, bless this food.
All: Come, Lord Jesus, come.

Second Sunday

Leader: Prepare the way of the Lord.
All: Make his paths straight.

Light two candles.

> LORD, DURING THIS ADVENT,
> help us to prepare your way
> by being kind and considerate,
> not thinking of ourselves first
> but of one another's needs.
> Thank you for this food that gives us strength.
> Amen.

Leader: Prepare the way of the Lord.
All: Make his paths straight.

Weekdays of the Second Week

Leader: Come, Lord Jesus, prepare our hearts.
All: Come, Lord Jesus, come.

Light two candles.

> LOVING GOD,
> you gave the prophet Isaiah a vision of peace,
> where the wolf is a guest of the lamb
> and the lion and calf graze together.
> May this meal strengthen us to prepare your way
> by making peace with one another

and all the creatures of this earth.
Thank you for this food we share,
bless it and bless us in Jesus' name we pray.
Amen.

Leader: Come, Lord Jesus, prepare our hearts.
All: Come, Lord Jesus, come.

Third Sunday

Leader: Rejoice in the Lord always.
All: Again, I say, rejoice.

Light three candles, including the pink one.

LORD, AS WE SHARE THIS MEAL,
fill us with the happiness that comes
from being kind and generous
and from serving you in others.
Thank you for this time together.
Amen.

Leader: Rejoice in the Lord always.
All: Again, I say, rejoice.

Weekdays of the Third Week

Leader: Come, Lord Jesus, give us joy.
All: Come, Lord Jesus, come.

Light three candles.

DEAR JESUS,
we are truly happy that your birthday is so near.

Help us to prepare for your coming
by responding to the call of St. John the Baptist
to be unselfish and patient with one another.
As we share this food,
teach us to share our hearts as well.
Amen.

Leader: Come, Lord Jesus, give us joy.
All: Come, Lord Jesus, come.

Fourth Sunday

Leader: Hail Mary, full of grace.
All: The Lord is with you.

Light four candles.

LORD, AS THE DAYS GROW SHORTER,
we remember that the day of your birth is near.
May the food and the love that we share around
this table
strengthen us to share your light with all those we meet.
Amen.

Leader: Hail Mary, full of grace.
All: The Lord is with you.

Weekdays of the Fourth Week

Leader: Come, Lord Jesus, be our light.
All: Come, Lord Jesus, come.

Light four candles.

FATHER,
thank you for the gift of Mary, our mother,
who said yes when you asked her
to become the mother of your Son, Jesus.
Help us to welcome him into our hearts
and into our family
as he comes to us this Christmas
and as he is with us now as we share this meal.
Amen.

Leader: Come, Lord Jesus, be our light.
All: Come, Lord Jesus, come.

Las Posadas

Las Posadas is a Mexican tradition that takes place during the nine days before Christmas, from December 16 to December 24. Families go from house to house playing the role of the pilgrims, Joseph and Mary. At each house they are turned away by the innkeepers. That family then joins the pilgrims and continues to the next house. At the last house, all are welcomed in and a joyful meal is shared. The following text is a translation of the traditional hymn that is sung. You can adapt it for use in your family, with each person taking a verse of the hymn.

Pilgrim:
In the name of heaven, I beg you for shelter.
My beloved wife and I can walk no farther.

Innkeeper:
This is not an inn, so be on your way.
I can't open the door for you, you might be a robber.

Pilgrim:
We've come all the way from Nazareth, and
we're exhausted.
My name is Joseph. I'm a carpenter.

Innkeeper:
I don't care what your name is! Let us sleep!
I've already told you, I'm not going to open the door.

Pilgrim:
My wife's name is Mary, the Queen of Heaven.
She's going to be the mother of the Divine Word.

Innkeeper:
Are you really Joseph? Is your wife really Mary?
Come in then! I didn't recognize you.

All:
Come in, holy pilgrims. Come in!
Welcome to our humble home.
Although it is a simple place,
we welcome you with all our hearts!

Las Posadas es una tradición mexicana que tiene lugar durante los nueve días antes de Navidad, del 16 al 24 de diciembre. Las familias van de casa en casa haciendo el papel de los peregrinos, José y Maria. En cada casa son rechazados por los posaderos. Luego, esa familia se une a los peregrinos y continúa a la siguiente casa. En la última casa todos son recibidos y se comparten una comida festiva. El siguiente texto es el himno tradicional que se canta. Ustedes pueden adaptarlo para usar en su familia con cada persona tomando un versículo del himno.

Peregrinos:
En nombre del cielo os pido posada,
pues no puede andar ya mi esposa amada.

Posaderos:
Aquí no es mesón, sigan adelante.
Yo no puedo abrir, no sea algún tunante.

Peregrinos:
Venimos rendidos desde Nazaret.
Yo soy carpintero de nombre José.

Posaderos:
No me importa el nombre, déjennos dormir,
pues que yo les digo que no hemos de abrir.

Peregrinos:
Mi esposa es María; es reina del cielo,
y madre va a ser del Divino Verbo.

Posaderos:
¿Eres tú José ¿Tu esposa es María?
Entren peregrinos, no los conocía.

Todos:
Entren santos peregrinos, reciban este rincón.
Aunque es pobre la morada, os la doy de corazón.

The Christmas Season

Christmas Eve

DEAR GOD,
as we gather together as a family (and with friends)
on this special night,
we remember how Mary and Joseph
came to Bethlehem seeking shelter
but found no place to stay.
As we begin our celebration of Jesus' birth,
help us, by our kindness and generosity,
to welcome him into our home.
Show us how to care for him
by caring for all those in need.
Bless this meal and our celebration this night.
Amen.

Christmas Day

LOVING FATHER,
on this special day, we thank you
for the gift of your Son, Jesus,
who was born into our world as a helpless baby.
We thank you for one another,
for the love we share,
and for the gifts we have exchanged
as signs of that love.
We remember those whom we love who are not with us today,
and ask you to bless us all.
We give you thanks
for this wonderful meal before us.

Make us generous and caring to all those in need.
Amen.

The Days after Christmas

GRACIOUS GOD,
we thank you for this joyful season,
for the warmth of family and friends,
and for the many gifts we have received from
your goodness.
Bless this meal and each of us who shares it.
Amen.

The Holy Family

The Sunday after Christmas

THANK YOU, LORD, FOR THE GIFT OF OUR FAMILY.
Help us to support one another by our love,
to encourage one another by our compliments,
and to forgive the hurts caused by our forgetfulness.
Bless this food,
and in everything we do, help us to be grateful.
Amen.

New Year's Eve

GENEROUS GOD,
as we look back on this past year,
we remember the people, places, and events
that were a part of our lives.
We recall that there were difficult times and good times.
And we know that through it all,
even when we did not realize it,
you were with us.
We thank you for your loving presence

and ask you to be with us once again
as we share this meal together.
Amen.

New Year's Day

GOD OF ALL HOPEFULNESS,
as we begin this new year,
we ask for the presence of your Holy Spirit
to guide and protect us.
We pray for good health in our family
and peace in our world.
And we thank you for the many blessings you give us,
especially for this food.
Amen.

Epiphany

The Sunday after New Year's Day

ALL LOVING GOD,
today we remember how you sent a bright star
to guide the wise men to Jesus.
As a sign of their love,
they offered him gifts of gold, frankincense, and myrrh.
Help us to follow our guiding stars
and to give generously from all we have received.
May this meal strengthen us on our journey
and bring us closer together in love.
Amen.

Lent

Ash Wednesday

GOD OF MERCY,
as we begin the season of Lent today,
we put on ashes to remember our sins
and turn to you for forgiveness.
During these forty days,
help us to pray more
and to keep our promises to make sacrifices
and to share with those in need.
Help us not to think so much about ourselves
but about others and you.
And bless this food we share.
Amen.

Lenten Weekdays

Monday

LORD JESUS,
you always reached out to those who sinned.
You drank water with the Samaritan woman
and shared bread with Zacchaeus.
Be with us now at this table.
Help us to turn away from sin
and be faithful to your Gospel.
Amen.

Tuesday

LOVING GOD,
as we gather for this meal,
we remember those who are hungry,

those who are homeless,
and those who are sick.
During this season of Lent,
help us always to find new ways
to care for them
and to share from what we have.
We thank you for this food.
Amen.

Wednesday

LORD JESUS,
you are the living water,
you are the bread of life,
you are the light of the world.
May the food and the love
we share at this meal
strengthen us
to give water to the thirsty,
bread to the hungry,
and light to those in darkness.
Amen.

Thursday

LORD GOD,
may everything we do
during this season of Lent
begin with your inspiration,
carry on with your help,
and reach its conclusion under your guidance.
Bless this meal we share
and teach us to be grateful for all your gifts.
Amen.

Friday

LORD JESUS,
we remember on this Friday
how you gave your life for us on the Cross.
Help us to show our gratitude
by remaining faithful to the Lenten practices
that we have begun.
Bless this food that we share in your name.
Amen.

Saturday

BLESSED ARE YOU, GOD OF OUR ANCESTORS.
For forty years you fed your people
with manna and quail as they wandered through
the desert.
Sustain us in our fasting and prayer
during these forty days of Lent
so that we may come at last to the joy of Easter.
Amen.

Lenten Sundays

First Sunday of Lent

DEAR JESUS,
you fasted for forty days and forty nights
and afterward you were hungry.
During this season of Lent,
help us to imitate you,
to give up something
so that we can think of others more.
Help us to be grateful for all we have,
especially for this meal,
which is a gift of your goodness.
Amen.

Second Sunday of Lent

LORD JESUS CHRIST,
we remember today how you brought your friends
Peter, James, and John to the top of a high mountain,
where your face dazzled like the sun
and your clothes were as bright as any light.
During this Lent,
help us to grow in friendship with you.
Fill our hearts with the brightness of your love
so that we can serve you and one another.
As we gather round this table,
we remember the words of Peter,
"Lord, it is good that we are here."

Third Sunday of Lent

JESUS, WE REMEMBER TODAY
how you came to the well in Samaria
feeling hungry and thirsty.
When you asked the woman for a drink,
she not only gave you water but also her heart.
As we come to this table,
we, too, are hungry and thirsty.
We ask you to nourish our bodies and our hearts
so that during this Lent we can grow in your love.
Amen.

Fourth Sunday of Lent

MERCIFUL FATHER,
today we remember the story of the prodigal son.
Like the forgiving father,
you set a wonderful banquet before us
when we turn from our sins and come home to you.
As we share this meal,

help us to learn how to forgive one another.
We thank you for this food
and for the gift of our family.
Amen.

Fifth Sunday of Lent

LORD JESUS,
you taught us that the grain of wheat must die
so that it could grow and produce much fruit.
As we see this food before us,
we remember that it has sprung from many seeds
that died to give new life.
Help us to remember that we are all like seeds:
our selfishness must die
so that we can grow in love.
Thank you for this food we share.
Amen.

Passion (Palm) Sunday

Leader: Hosanna in the highest.
All: Hosanna in the highest.

LORD JESUS,
although you were a king, you rode on a donkey.
The people praised you
but they did not follow your Word.
As we begin this Holy Week,
help us to praise you not only in our words
but also in our deeds.
Strengthen us through this meal we now share.

Leader: Blessed is the one who comes in the name of the Lord.
All: Hosanna in the highest.

The Triduum

Holy Thursday

Dear Jesus,
today we remember
how you shared your last supper with your friends.
You gave them bread and wine saying,
"This is my Body. This is my Blood."
And after dinner, you washed their feet.
We thank you
for the gift of your presence in the Eucharist
and for teaching us how to care for one another.
As we share this meal,
help us to imitate your generous love
by giving from our hearts to one another
and all in need.
Amen.

Good Friday

Lord Jesus Christ,
on this most holy day, you gave your life on the Cross
to show us how much you love us.
In the midst of your suffering,
you forgave those who were crucifying you,
and you placed your life in your Father's hands.
As we share this simple meal,
we remember your love.
We ask you to help us grow in forgiveness and trust,
and to recognize you
in all those who are suffering today.
Amen.

Holy Saturday

LORD JESUS,
when you died on the Cross,
your friends and followers were saddened and shocked.
But three days later,
the Father raised you up to new life, and they rejoiced.
As we prepare to celebrate Easter,
help us to remember its true meaning in our lives.
May we never give up hope
and rejoice always in your presence with us.
Bless this meal that we share together.
Amen.

The Easter Season

Easter and the Sundays of the Easter Season

Leader: Jesus Christ is risen today.
All: Alleluia.
Leader: We rejoice and are glad.
All: Alleluia.

LORD JESUS,
we celebrate your resurrection
and we rejoice in your love.
You are with us now as we share this meal,
offering us forgiveness, peace, and new life.
Help us to recognize you in the breaking of this bread,
and strengthen us to share
the good news of your rising with others.

Leader: Jesus Christ is risen today.
All: Alleluia.
Leader: We rejoice and are glad.
All: Alleluia.

Easter Weekdays

LORD JESUS,
you are the bread of life,
you are the living water.
You are the Good Shepherd,
who prepares a banquet for us
and fills our cups to overflowing.
May this meal nourish our bodies

and may your presence here among us renew
our spirits.
Strengthen us to serve you in one another
and especially in the poor.
We ask this in faith.
Amen.

Divine Mercy Sunday

The Sunday after Easter

LORD JESUS,
we remember how on the day of your resurrection
you said to your apostles, "Peace be with you,"
and you sent them to forgive sins.
One week later, Thomas placed his hand in
your wounds
and cried, "My Lord and my God."
On this Divine Mercy Sunday,
we thank you for forgiving our sins
and for calling us to touch your wounds
when we care for those who are suffering.
We are happy that you are here with us at this table.
Help us to remember that you are with us always—
whatever we do, wherever we go.

Ascension Thursday

JESUS, RISEN LORD,
as you ascended into heaven
you said to your disciples,
"And behold, I am with you always, until the end of
the age."
Be with us as we seek
to share your love with all those we meet,
and be present at our table

to strengthen and renew us.
May this meal be a sign
of our love for one another,
and may it strengthen us
to follow your call.
Amen.

Pentecost

Leader: Come, Holy Spirit.
All: Renew the hearts of your people.

GRACIOUS GOD,
you sent the Holy Spirit
upon the frightened disciples
to renew their faith
and strengthen their courage
to preach the Gospel of your Son, Jesus.
As we share this meal together,
send your Spirit upon us.
Renew us with your love
and strengthen us by your Spirit's presence
to be signs of hope for those around us.

Leader: Come, Holy Spirit.
All: Renew the hearts of your people.

Ordinary Time

Trinity Sunday

The Sunday after Pentecost

LOVING FATHER,
you sent us your Son, Jesus,
to be the way, the truth, and the life.
You gave us your Holy Spirit
to guide us and fill us with Christ's love.
You are one God, three persons!
Help us to share more deeply
in your boundless love as the Trinity.
May our family be a reflection of that love.
We ask you to bless this meal
and make this prayer
in the name of the Father, the Son, and the Holy Spirit.
Amen.

All should make the Sign of the Cross.

The Body and Blood of Christ

The Sunday after Trinity Sunday

LORD JESUS,
you are the bread of life!
When we receive you in bread and wine,
you are present to us in the most real way possible.
Help us to grow in our love for you
present in the Eucharist.
As we gather around this table,

we know that you are here with us too.
Let us show our love for you
by the way we treat and care for one another.
Let us show our thanks for this meal
by the way we share our riches with others.
Amen.

Holidays and Saints' Days through the Year

January 4: St. Elizabeth Seton

Elizabeth Seton is the first native-born American saint. A mother of five children, she was twenty-seven years old when her husband died. She converted to Catholicism and began the religious order the Sisters of Charity of St. Joseph. She founded a number of schools in Maryland and also worked with orphans and the sick.

Loving God,
we remember today the life of St. Elizabeth Seton,
a mother, a teacher,
and a compassionate friend
to orphans and the sick.
As we share this meal together,
help us to remember and be grateful
for all those who care for us,
especially our teachers.
As we return to school after Christmas vacation,
make us aware of the gifts we have
to share with others—
the gifts of knowledge,
the gifts of friendship,
and the gifts of our helping hands to those in need.
We ask you to bless this food in Jesus' name.
Amen.

January 5: St. John Neumann

John Neumann came to America from his home in Bohemia in 1835 at the age of twenty-four. He had just one suit of clothes and only a dollar. He was ordained a priest the next year and worked in New York and Pennsylvania. He eventually became the bishop of Philadelphia, where he worked especially hard to open many Catholic schools.

DEAR GOD,
as we remember St. John Neumann,
we ask you to give us strength
to be true to our callings.
Just as he followed his dream
to serve you in America,
help us to follow your voice
wherever it may lead us.
We thank you for this food we share.
Help us not to take it
or any of your gifts for granted.
We ask this in Jesus' name.
Amen.

January 6: St. André Bessette

André Bessette came from a family of twelve children. His father, a carpenter and lumberjack in a small town in Canada, died when a tree fell on him. Just three years later, André's mother died of tuberculosis. At the age of twelve André left home for the United States to find work. But after a few years he returned and his pastor helped him join the Holy Cross Brothers. He was given the name André, and because of his lack of education, he was assigned to be the doorkeeper at Notre Dame College in Montreal. Br. André also gave haircuts for five cents and eventually saved enough money to build a little chapel to St. Joseph. Many who were sick came there to ask Br. André to pray with them for healing, and they recovered. People wanted to give him the credit, but he always said, "I do not cure. St. Joseph cures."

Dear Jesus,
you were Brother André's constant companion.
You gave him hope when he became an orphan,
and you gave him a special love for your
    foster-father, Joseph.
Today we remember how he humbly served you
as a doorkeeper, a barber, and a friend to the sick.
Be with us so we can overcome the hardships we face
and be generous and grateful for what we receive,
especially this meal that we now share.
Amen.

Martin Luther King Jr. Day

The Third Monday of January

Martin Luther King Jr., the great leader of the civil rights movement, was born in Atlanta, Georgia, on January 15, 1929. Like his father and grandfather, he was a minister and an eloquent preacher. Dr. King came to national attention in December of 1955 when he organized a boycott of the Montgomery, Alabama, bus system after Rosa Parks was jailed for refusing to give up her seat to a white man. He is perhaps best remembered for his "I Have a Dream" speech, given before 250,000 people in August of 1963 at the March on Washington to demonstrate for equal rights for African Americans. On April 4, 1968, Dr. King was assassinated in Memphis, Tennessee, a victim of the hatred he had spoken so forcefully against.

O GOD OF JUSTICE,
you raised up Martin Luther King Jr.
as a voice crying in the wilderness
for peace and harmony among all races and creeds.
Help us to dream his dream of freedom and equality.
Help us to remove all prejudice in ourselves
and to right the wrongs caused by ignorance and fear.
Teach us how to share our bread
with those who are oppressed,
and bless this food
that we share in your name.
Amen.

January 24: St. Francis de Sales

Francis was born in Chateaux de Sales, a town in the Alpine mountains of France, in 1567. He came from a wealthy family, and his parents wanted him to become a lawyer. Near the end of his studies he realized that God was calling him to be a priest. Although this caused quite an uproar in his family, Francis became a priest and volunteered to work in an area of Switzerland that was hostile to Catholics. This was the time of the Reformation, and Catholics and Protestants were bitterly divided. But Francis worked to win over people not through arguing but through preaching Jesus' message of love. In his famous book *Introduction to the Devout Life,* he teaches that the way to follow Jesus is through gentle love and service in our everyday lives. He wrote, "The measure of love is to love without measure."

DEAR GOD,
help us to imitate St. Francis de Sales,
not by arguing with others
but by treating them with kindness.
Teach us how to serve
our family, friends, and all those we meet
by thinking of their needs
and being generous in how we help them.
Send us your Holy Spirit to help us be better writers
and to use whatever talents we have to serve you.
We ask this in the name of Jesus, our Lord.
Amen.

January 25: Conversion of St. Paul

Before he became a believer, Paul was a fierce persecutor of the Church, feared by Christians everywhere. He even stood by and approved as St. Stephen, the first martyr, was stoned to death. One day, as he was riding his horse on a journey to Damascus to persecute Christians there, Jesus appeared to him and asked, "Why are you persecuting me?" (This story is found in Acts 9.) Paul not only became a Christian but also traveled throughout the world teaching about Christ.

LORD JESUS CHRIST,
the bright light of your presence
changed the fear and hatred in Paul's heart
to love and compassion.
May the same light of your love
be with us at this table.
Let it calm our fears
and mend the hurts that divide us.
May this food strengthen us
to be signs of your presence
in our words and deeds.
Amen.

January 26: Sts. Timothy and Titus

Timothy and Titus were companions of Paul on his journeys, and they helped him preach the Gospel to the cities where they went by ship. They were missionaries who lived an adventurous and exciting life. Timothy was a favorite disciple of Paul. When Paul was twice put in prison for preaching the Gospel, Timothy visited him and took care of him. Titus was also a trusted disciple of Paul. He helped Paul settle the problems that were occurring in the church in the city of Corinth. Paul wrote two letters to Timothy and one to Titus that are part of the New Testament. In each of these letters he calls them his true children in faith since they became Christians because of his preaching.

DEAR GOD,
you gave Paul, Timothy, and Titus the gift of faith
and filled them with much courage and energy
to preach the Gospel
even when it was very hard for them.
We ask you to give us the faith and strength
to share the Good News of your love
by our words and example.
Help us to be good friends,
as Timothy and Titus were to Paul.
May this meal give us strength,
and may this time together as a family
help us to grow in our faith and love.
Amen.

January 28: St. Thomas Aquinas

Thomas was born into a well-off family in southern Italy in 1225. Because he was the fourth son, his parents followed a custom of that time and sent him to live in a monastery. Thomas was happy there, but as he grew older he decided that he wanted to join the Dominicans, a religious order that traveled about preaching. His parents were so upset that they kidnapped him and locked him up for a year in their castle. Thomas would not give up, and they eventually let him go. He went to the university in Cologne, Germany, to study theology. Because he was very quiet and rather heavy, his classmates called him "the dumb ox." But Thomas was actually brilliant and eventually became the greatest theologian in the history of the Church. Near the end of his life, Thomas had a spiritual experience that led him to say, "I cannot go on. All that I have written seems like so much straw compared to what I have seen."

HOLY AND LOVING GOD,
you gave St. Thomas Aquinas a brilliant mind
and a strong will to overcome all the obstacles he faced.
Help us to use the brains you have given us
to work hard at our studies and not to give up,
even if others make fun of us or don't believe in us.
Give us the wisdom to know that your love for each of us
is greater than we can ever imagine.
We thank you for this meal and for all that we have.
Amen.

Chinese New Year

Late January or Early February

The date of Chinese New Year is determined by the lunar calendar, so it varies from year to year. The Chinese divide the years into cycles of twelve, with each year being named for an animal. The New Year is celebrated with a festive meal, parades, and fireworks.

GOD OF ALL PEOPLE,
as we remember Chinese New Year,
help us to be aware that all people—
of every race, language, and country—
are your children.
Help us to appreciate the differences among us
and learn from one another.
Show us your face in the smiles and laughter
of children everywhere.
Thank you for this meal
and for this special day.
Amen.

Super Bowl Sunday

Sunday in February

The Super Bowl was first played in 1967 in Los Angeles. That game pitted the Green Bay Packers against the Kansas City Chiefs. The Packers won. Though not an officially recognized holiday, many Americans gather together on Super Bowl Sunday with family, friends, and neighbors to share a meal before or during the game.

ALMIGHTY GOD,
you give us this day of rest and relaxation,
this time to enjoy the Super Bowl together.
We thank you for all your gifts
and for this good food that we share.
As you have blessed these athletes with strength
and agility,
give us the energy and wisdom that we need
to be faithful in the calling
you have given to each of us.
We ask this through Christ, our Lord.
Amen.

February 1: St. Brigid

Brigid grew up as a slave in Ireland. Despite this, she was so devoted to caring for the needs of others that she would give away her master's food and possessions. When he couldn't stop her, he realized it was better to set her free. Brigid became a nun and started a monastery in which there was a fire that, according to a legend, burned continuously for five hundred years without creating any ashes. There are many other stories of Brigid performing healings and miracles. In one story, she turned water into milk that cured a woman of leprosy. In another, she supplied beer to eighteen churches from one barrel for more than fifty days! While these stories may not all be true, they remind us that love and compassion are the most important virtues. The Gospel tells us that whatever we do for the least of Jesus' brothers and sisters, we do for him.

Dear God,
the fire of your love burns within us.
Let it warm our hearts in the midst of winter
to remember those who are cold, hungry, or sick.
Help us to follow St. Brigid's example of generosity
and to share what we have with those in need.
We thank you for this good food that we share
and the warmth of our home.
Amen.

February 2: The Presentation of the Lord

Today we remember how Joseph and Mary brought Jesus to the Temple in Jerusalem. According to Jewish custom, Mary was to be purified forty days after giving birth to a son. In Luke 2:22–38, we read how they made the customary offering of the poor—two turtledoves—and then heard the prophetic words of Anna and Simeon.

Today is also the midpoint between the first day of winter and the first day of spring. For this reason, many popular customs have grown up around it. One of the customs is the blessing of candles, whose light illuminates the winter nights. And as everyone knows, it is Groundhog Day. We watch to see if the groundhog sees its shadow and find out how many more days of winter there will be.

GOD OF ALL HOPEFULNESS,
you sent your child, Jesus,
as a light shining in the darkness
to fulfill the longings of your people.
As we rejoice in his coming,
we look for the light of his presence in our lives
and the warmth of his love in our home.
May this meal we share renew us in this wintry season.
May it strengthen us to hasten
the springtime of your reign among us.
Amen.

February 3: St. Blaise

Blaise grew up in the small country of Armenia. We don't know too much about his life, but we do know that he was a bishop during a time when Christians were persecuted by the Romans, and that he was a martyr. He was a very popular saint during the Middle Ages, and there were many stories told about him. Blaise was arrested by the governor, who made him live in a cave. One story tells how injured animals would come to him and he would heal them. Another was about a mother whose son was choking on a fish bone stuck in his throat. Blaise prayed for him and made the Sign of the Cross, and the boy recovered. St. Blaise became the patron of people with throat diseases or just plain sore throats. That's why today a priest will bless your throat by holding two crossed candles to your throat and praying for your health.

Dear Jesus,
during your life you healed many who were sick.
Your healing love continues for us in our Church and in our family today.
As we share this meal, we remember how St. Blaise continued your work
as a bishop and a healer and gave his life for his faith.
We pray for all who are sick,
especially those with sore throats,
and ask you to give us the patience and faith we need
when we are sick too.
Amen.

February 4: Rosa Parks

Today is the birthday of Rosa Parks, a courageous leader in the civil rights movement in the 1950s and 1960s. After her parents separated, Rosa lived on a farm with her grandparents, her mother, and her brother. She had to leave school while still in high school to take care of her grandmother and then her mother. Rosa was a seamstress, and she worked in a department store in Montgomery, Alabama. One day she was riding on a bus, seated in the "colored section." Black people were not allowed to sit where white people sat. When the driver ordered her to give up her seat to a white man, she refused. Rosa was arrested, and the black community responded by boycotting the buses for more than a year. Her lawsuit protesting the arrest went all the way to the Supreme Court and resulted in a decision that bus segregation was illegal. Rosa Parks is considered "the first lady of civil rights," and there is a statue of her in the United States Capitol.

Dear God,
help us to recognize the dignity of each person,
no matter what race or religion he or she is.
We are all your children
and so we are all equal before you.
Give us the courage to stand up for what is right
when we see something wrong happening.
Thank you for the gifts you have given to each of us.
Please bless this meal
and make us strong and brave in doing what is right.
Amen.

February 8: St. Josephine Bakhita

Josephine Bakhita was born in 1869 in a small village in Sudan in Africa, where her uncle was the chief. At first she had a happy life in a loving family of seven children. But one day when she was about seven years old, she was kidnapped while working in the fields. The slave traders made her walk barefoot for six hundred miles to a city where she was sold to a very cruel master. In all, she was sold five times and was tortured many times by her various owners. Finally she was bought by an Italian government official. He was kinder to her and after two years gave her to his friend to be a nanny. When the man's daughter went to school in Italy, Josephine went with her. There she met the sisters who ran the school. They helped her win her freedom, and she was baptized and joined their community. As a sister, she did cooking, sewing, and embroidery. She was loved for her kindness and holiness by the children at the school and all the local citizens.

LOVING FATHER,
through all of her suffering you were always with St.
Josephine Bakhita.
You comforted her when she was frightened
and gave her hope when things seemed hopeless.
Help us to follow her example and trust in your care
when we feel frightened or alone.
We thank you for the love of our family
and for this meal that we share together.
Amen.

February 11: Our Lady of Lourdes

On this day in 1858, the Blessed Mother first appeared to a fourteen-year-old girl named Bernadette in Lourdes, France. During the next five months, Mary appeared to her eighteen times and told her that a church should be built there. Many people came to the place and were cured of their illnesses. Today people travel from all over the world to Lourdes and many are healed there.

LORD JESUS,
through the compassion of Mary, your mother,
you pour out your healing grace to the world.
Send your healing upon us and cure our illnesses.
Give us compassionate hearts for those who are sick.
Bless this meal we share,
and through the love of your mother,
guide us to reach out to the sick
and to all those who need us.
Amen.

February 14: Valentine's Day

The name of this day comes from St. Valentine, a priest who was martyred by the Roman emperor Claudius II around the year 269. The custom of sending valentines on this day began in medieval times. On this day in mild climates around the Mediterranean Sea, birds would choose their mates.

GOD OF LOVE,
we thank you for all the people
who love and care for us,
especially our families.
Help us to show our love in return.
May the valentines we share today
be signs of sincere love,
and may this meal bring us closer together.
We ask you to bless this food
and to be with those who
may feel lonely or forgotten today.
Amen.

Presidents' Day

The Third Monday of February

Today we celebrate two of our greatest presidents, George Washington and Abraham Lincoln. George Washington was born in Virginia on February 23, 1732. He was commander in chief of the colonial army during the Revolutionary War. On April 20, 1789, he became the first president of the United States. As he took the oath of office, his hand rested on the Bible, opened to Psalm 127: "Unless the LORD build the house, they labor in vain who build it."

Abraham Lincoln was born in Kentucky on February 12, 1804. As the sixteenth president of the United States, Lincoln sought to preserve the union during the American Civil War. In 1863, he issued the Emancipation Proclamation to free all slaves. He was assassinated on April 14, 1865, at the Ford's Theatre in Washington, DC.

GOD OF JUSTICE,
you inspired George Washington and Abraham Lincoln
to help create a nation where all men and women,
regardless of race or religion,
could live in freedom and equality.
Help us to remember their ideals
and to root our own efforts to do good in your justice.
Bless this meal, and through it, give us strength
to work for what is right and just.
Amen.

February 25: Bl. Rani Mariam Vattalil

Mariam Vattalil was born in Kerala, India, in 1954. When she graduated from high school, she joined the Franciscan sisters and received the name Rani. Rani means "queen," so the name was in honor of the Blessed Mother. She was very outspoken on behalf of the poor and landless people. Some wealthy landlords were so outraged at this that they hired a group of thugs to stab her to death while she was riding on a bus. The leader, Jeevan Singh, was sent to prison for life. But Rani's sister and mother each visited him and forgave him. He begged their forgiveness and was eventually released from prison. Sr. Rani's family welcomed him as one of their own, and he was present at her beatification in 2017.

Lord Jesus,
you gave us the greatest example
of love and forgiveness
as you hung on the Cross and prayed,
"Father, forgive them, they know not what they do."
We thank you for the amazing example
of Bl. Rani Mariam Vattalil.
Help us to imitate her care for the poor,
to follow her family's example of forgiveness.
We remember the poor in India and our own country
and ask you to guide us to care for them.
Thank you for this food and all the blessings we enjoy.
Amen.

March 3: St. Katharine Drexel

Katharine Drexel was a rich girl. Her father was a wealthy banker, and she and her sisters had the best of everything, from private tutors to their own railroad car! But they also received a wonderful spiritual formation. Her stepmother welcomed the poor into their mansion three days a week, and she provided food, clothing, and help with rent. Her father prayed for a half hour every evening. On a trip to the Dakotas, Katharine saw for the first time the poverty of the Sioux people there and she was moved to help them. Eventually she became a nun and founded the Sisters of the Blessed Sacrament, an order dedicated to Native Americans and African Americans. She used millions of dollars that she inherited to establish many schools for Native American children. And she founded Xavier University in New Orleans.

LORD JESUS,
through the example of her family,
you gave St. Katharine Drexel a love for the poor.
You inspired her to let go
of a life of privilege and wealth to help others.
We thank you, Lord, for what we have,
and we remember that you have blessed us
with so much, while many others have so little.
Help us to be grateful for all that we have received
and for this meal before us.
Amen.

March 12: St. Joseph Zhang Dapeng

Joseph Zhang Dapeng was born in China around 1754. He made and sold silk for a living. When he was about forty years old, he heard about Christianity from another person in his business and he soon was baptized, even though his family and friends were against it. His business associates forced him to leave the company, and so he opened a new store on his own. He began preaching and teaching, and he turned his store into a small school. When the government started to persecute Christians, he went into hiding but he still continued to preach. But his brother-in-law betrayed him, and he was arrested. On March 12, 1815, he was put to death at the age of sixty-one.

Dear Father,
your Holy Spirit guided St. Joseph Zhang Dapeng
  through many changes in his life.
You led him to discover the Gospel through a friend,
and when others rejected him for his faith,
you guided him to a new life of preaching and teaching.
Even when someone in his family betrayed him,
you gave him the patience and strength to continue.
Today we remember all of the Catholic people
in China and in our country
who have a special love for St. Joseph.
Help us to follow you wherever you lead us
and to have grateful hearts for all your gifts,
especially for this meal that we now share.
Amen.

March 15: St. Louise de Marillac

Louise de Marillac never knew her mother, who died when she was a baby. Her father was a wealthy man who took good care of her. But when he married a new wife, she was sent to a convent boarding school where her aunt was a nun. When she was fifteen, her father also died, and Louise had to live in a boarding house. After a while, her uncle arranged for her to marry. Although she wanted to become a nun, she got married. She and her husband were happy together and had a son. But when her husband died, she decided to devote herself to serving God. Soon she met a priest, Vincent de Paul, and joined him and a group of wealthy women in working with the poor in Paris. Eventually she started a community of women called the Daughters of Charity who lived and worked among the poor caring for their needs. This was something entirely new; before then, nuns lived in convents and did not go out among the people.

LOVING GOD,
you guided St. Louise de Marillac through the many twists and turns of her life.
You consoled her when family members died
and showed her a new way to serve you in caring for the poor.
Help us to remember that you are always with us
and give us the same desire as St. Louise to serve you,
especially in caring for those in need.
Amen.

March 17: St. Patrick's Day

St. Patrick is the patron saint of Ireland and is special to all people of Irish descent. He was born around the year 389 and first came to Ireland at about the age of sixteen, when he was carried there as a slave by pirates. After six years he escaped, but soon heard the call of God to go back as a missionary. After being ordained a bishop, he returned to Ireland, where he converted the Celtic chiefs and people throughout the land.

Christ be with us,
be within us.
Christ beside us,
behind, and before us.
Christ to comfort us,
to nourish and strengthen us.
Christ in the hungry,
the weak, and the lonely.
Christ among us,
to feed and send us.
Amen.

Based on The Breastplate of St. Patrick.

March 19: St. Joseph

Joseph, the husband of Mary and the foster-father of Jesus, played a key role in the events of Jesus' birth. Twice he received a message from God in a dream, telling him not to be afraid to take Mary as his wife and then warning him to flee to Egypt to escape King Herod's jealous wrath.

Joseph was a carpenter and taught this trade to Jesus. Because he is not mentioned during Jesus' public life, Christians have always believed that he must have died before then. Joseph is especially revered by people of Italian descent, who celebrate this day with special foods.

GOD OF LOVE,
you chose St. Joseph to be the foster-father of Jesus,
and through him taught Jesus to call you
"Abba" (Daddy).
We thank you for Joseph's strong faith and
constant care.
Help us to grow in faith and love
and to be grateful for all the gifts you give us,
especially for this meal that we bless in Christ's name.
Amen.

First Day of Spring

GOD OF NEW LIFE,
we give you praise and thanks
for this first day of spring.
We thank you for sustaining us through the winter
and for the returning warmth of the sun.
We praise you for the new life
that springs from the earth—
for the food that nourishes our bodies
and for the flowers that gladden our hearts.
Bless this meal that we share.
May we, too, be signs of new life
and hope for our world.
Amen.

March 24: St. Óscar Romero

When Óscar Romero was chosen as archbishop of San Salvador, the capital of El Salvador, no one expected him to become the champion of the poor and oppressed in his country. He had been a rather conservative and quiet priest and bishop. But when his friend Fr. Rutilio Grande was murdered for speaking out against the oppression of the poor, Óscar Romero experienced a profound conversion. He became a vocal critic of the government that was oppressing the poor and often killing them when they had done nothing wrong. Many priests and people were arrested, tortured, and killed. In a sermon delivered on March 23, 1980, Romero pleaded with the soldiers not to obey commands to kill innocent people, but to obey God's law. The very next day he was shot by an assassin while celebrating Mass. He died at the altar.

O GOD OF JUSTICE AND MERCY,
you filled St. Óscar Romero with the courage
  and strength
to speak out against the greed and hatred
that were bringing so much suffering to his people.
Help us to recognize the suffering of the poor
and to do whatever we can for them.
You have blessed us with an abundance of good things.
Help us to show our gratitude
by sharing with others
and working to make their lives better.
Amen.

March 25: The Annunciation

Chapter 1 of St. Luke's gospel tells us how the angel Gabriel announced to Mary that she was to be the mother of the long-awaited Messiah. Gabriel's words form the first part of the Hail Mary: "Hail Mary, full of grace, the Lord is with you. Blessed are you among women." Mary said in reply, "May it be done to me according to your word" (Lk 1:38).

LORD GOD,
you sent the angel Gabriel to announce to Mary
that she would be the mother of your Son.
Today we remember her trust in your Word
and her faith in your promise.
As she said yes to you,
help us to do your will in all things each day.
Bless this meal that we share,
and keep our hearts and minds open
to the unexpected ways
that you speak to us through one another.
We ask this through Jesus, our Lord.
Amen.

April 1: April Fool's Day

Today is a day to play tricks and try to fool one another. There are many ideas about how this custom began, although no one knows exactly how it got started. One story goes that it was on this day that Noah was fooled by the weather and mistakenly sent out a dove to look for land. This day once was the first day of spring (before the calendar was corrected), and spring is certainly a season when we, like Noah, can find that the weather plays tricks on us!

O God, our Creator,
we thank you for the joy of this spring season
and for the many fun times we share together.
Help us to make one another happy—
to laugh, to smile, and to play together.
Bless this food.
Make this and every meal
a time to rejoice in your love.
Amen.

April 12: St. Teresa of the Andes

Juana Fernández Solar was not a well-behaved child. Born on July 13, 1900, she came from a wealthy family in Santiago, Chile. Although she was generous and prayed often, she was moody, stuck-up, and easily angered. But after reading the autobiography of St. Thérèse of Lisieux, Juana changed. She decided to become a nun like Thérèse. She entered the convent and was given the name Teresa, after St. Thérèse. As she was preparing to become a sister, she wrote many letters sharing her experience of prayer and what Jesus had done for her. Sadly, Teresa became ill with typhus. She made her final vows as a sister just before she died in 1920 at the age of nineteen.

> Lord Jesus,
> we remember that you have loved us
> from the first moment of our lives until now,
> and that your love never changes,
> even when we do not act as we should.
> As we remember St. Teresa,
> we thank you for your constant love and patience
> with us.
> Help us to remember how much you love and care
> for us,
> to live lives of devotion to you,
> and to care for one another.
> And thank you for this food that we now share.
> Amen.

April 22: Earth Day

Since it was first observed on April 22, 1970, Earth Day has grown in popularity as we have become more and more aware of the fragile state of the environment. For those of us in the Northern Hemisphere, it comes at a time when spring is entering its fullness. It is a good day to be grateful for God's gifts and to renew our commitment to preserve them for the future.

GOD OF ALL CREATION,
as the life of spring grows all around us,
we give you thanks for the beauty of our world,
for sun and rain,
for flowers and crops.
As we share in the bounty of the land,
help us to grow in respect for the earth
and to preserve it for all people.
Bless this food we share,
a gift of your love
and the fruit of your creation.
Amen.

April 25: St. Mark

Although St. Mark's gospel comes second in the New Testament, scholars believe that it was actually the first to be written. Mark was a companion of Peter, and his gospel probably reflects what Peter taught him about the life and teaching of Jesus. Mark also traveled with Paul and Barnabas as a missionary. His gospel especially emphasizes Jesus' suffering and calls us to follow Jesus, even when it is difficult.

GRACIOUS GOD,
through the Holy Spirit
you inspired St. Mark to write the first gospel.
We thank you for the gift of your Word,
which teaches and nourishes us.
As you feed us through the scripture,
strengthen us with this food.
May your Spirit inspire us
to share the Good News with others.
Amen.

April 29: St. Catherine of Siena

Catherine was the second youngest in a family of twenty-five children. She lived in Siena, Italy, during the fourteenth century. When Catherine was sixteen, her older sister died in childbirth. Her parents wanted her to marry her sister's husband, but she refused. In protest, she wouldn't eat, and she cut off her long hair. Catherine didn't want to marry or become a nun. She had a unique plan of her own. She persuaded the Dominican sisters to make her a member as a layperson. She lived at home and would give away her family's food and clothing to the poor without asking them! When she was twenty-one, she had a vison of Jesus, who told her to devote herself to caring for the poor and the sick. Catherine attracted many followers, and she even became an adviser to the pope.

DEAR JESUS,
you blessed St. Catherine with a determined spirit and
a deep love for you.
Help each of us to find our own way to love and
serve you
and to have the courage to be who you call us to be.
We are grateful for this food.
Teach us how to be generous with what we have,
especially with those who are poor, hungry, or in any
kind of need.
Amen.

May 1: St. Joseph the Worker

Today is the midpoint of spring, when the beauty and life of the season are in full bloom. Through the centuries this day has been celebrated as a day of new life—a joyful day to affirm the gifts of love and work. Our Christian calendar reminds us of St. Joseph, whose love and work sustained Mary and Jesus.

Bountiful God,
we thank you for all your gifts to us:
for the gift of spring,
with its warmth, light, and flowers;
for the gift of our work,
which challenges, supports, and fulfills us;
and for the gift of love,
with its kindness, patience, and forgiveness.
Bless this meal that we now share:
a gift from your goodness,
a reward for our labors,
and a sign of your love.
Amen.

May 3: Sts. Philip and James

Philip and James were two of Jesus' apostles. Philip, who came from the same town as Peter and Andrew, was one of the first disciples that Jesus called to follow him. Right away, Philip hurried to his friend Nathanael and told him to "come and see" Jesus. At the Last Supper, Philip asked Jesus, "Show us the Father." Jesus replied that if we see him, we see the Father too. There were actually two apostles named James. The James we celebrate today is sometimes called "James the Less," perhaps because he was short in height. The other James was the brother of John.

DEAR JESUS,
you call us, just as you called Philip and James,
to follow you and be your friends.
Help us to have the same enthusiasm as Philip
and to share your friendship with our own friends.
Help us, like James, to know how much you love us
whether we are tall or short,
and with whatever gifts or challenges we face.
Thank you for this meal
and for being here with us now
as we share it in your friendship.
Amen.

May 5: Cinco de Mayo

Cinco de Mayo, a national holiday in Mexico, is celebrated as a day of national pride by Mexican Americans throughout the United States. On May 5, 1862, a small Mexican force defeated an invading French army, which was twice their size, at the Battle of Puebla. Although the French soon triumphed and installed a puppet king in Mexico, he was eventually ousted in 1867.

GOD OF POWER AND MERCY,
as we pray for and with the people of Mexico,
we thank you for the gift of freedom.
We thank you for this day of fiesta
and for the gift of this food.
We remember all those who are hungry
as well as those who are not free.
Show us the way to bring your love to all people.
We ask this in Jesus' name.
Amen.

May 10: St. Damien of Molokai

Leprosy is a contagious disease that causes terrible sores on the skin and can be fatal. Until recent times, people with leprosy were kept away from others and often lived together in awful conditions. Jesus cured many lepers and they were able to return to their families. Today leprosy can be cured, but when Damien went as a missionary to Hawaii in 1864, there was not yet a cure. People with leprosy were taken from their families and sent to the faraway island of Molokai, where they had to live in caves and shacks. There were no doctors or people to care for them there. Fr. Damien volunteered to go to Molokai. He built a church there and for fifteen years worked alongside people to build houses, clinics, and schools. He called them his brothers and sisters. Eventually, in 1888, he died from the disease.

LORD JESUS, YOU WERE NOT AFRAID TO TOUCH LEPERS,
but healed them and gave them back to their families.
Help us to imitate you and St. Damien
by reaching out to others
who are alone or left out because they are different.
Help us not to be afraid to befriend them.
We thank you for this meal
and for the love and acceptance of our family.
Amen.

May 13: Our Lady of Fatima

Francisco Marto and his sister Jacinta were nine and seven, and their cousin Lucia Santos was ten, when the Blessed Mother appeared to them on May 13, 1917. They were looking after sheep in the hills near the town of Fatima in Portugal. They described her as a "Lady more brilliant than the sun." Mary asked the children to learn to read and write so they could better tell of her appearance, and to pray the Rosary to bring peace to the world and an end to World War I. She appeared to them on the thirteenth of each month for five more months. Each time more and more people came to see the appearances, but only the children could see her. By October 13, 1917, the date of her last appearance, more than thirty thousand people gathered and witnessed "the miracle of the sun," in which the sky was filled with brilliant colors and the sun appeared to dance around.

Dear Jesus,
thank you for sending us your mother,
who gave her message to pray for peace
to three young and poor children in Fatima, Portugal.
Help us to remember that no matter how young or old
we are,
you call us to be messengers of peace.
Please bless this meal
and be with those who suffer from war this day.
Amen.

Mother's Day

The Second Sunday in May

O GOD,
we thank you for giving us Mom
and for the many ways she shows us your
motherly love.
On this her special day, we ask you
to bless her with your joy and peace.
As she cares for all of us,
help her to find strength for the many challenges
she faces.
Help us to show our gratitude for all she does
and especially for who she is.
Bless this meal that we share in celebration of Mom,
and be with all mothers and grandmothers on this day.
Amen.

May 21: Bl. Franz Jägerstätter

Franz Jägerstätter was born in Austria on May 21, 1907. As a young man, Franz loved to ride his motorcycle, and he had a reputation as a wild youth. When he inherited his foster-father's farm, he returned home and married. His wife, Franziska, was very religious, and Franz began to study the Bible and the lives of the saints. They had three daughters. When the German army took over in Austria, Franz had to go to military training. Franz became aware of the horrible things the Nazis were doing and he objected to serving. He consulted his pastor and even traveled to talk with his bishop. They all told him he had an obligation to serve. But when he was finally called to active duty, he refused. He was arrested and imprisoned. He said, "I can only follow my conscience. . . . I know that, if I do what God wants me to do, he will take care of my family." On August 9, 1943, he was put to death.

O GOD, WE THANK YOU FOR THE EXAMPLE OF BL. FRANZ JÄGERSTÄTTER.
You gave him the courage to follow his conscience
no matter what might happen.
Help us to know what you call us to do
and give us the courage to listen to our conscience
when we face difficult choices.
Please bless this meal and be with those who suffer for following you.
Amen.

May 30: St. Joan of Arc

Joan could not read or write, but when she was twelve years old she had a vision and heard voices. She said it was St. Michael the Archangel, St. Catherine, and St. Margaret, and that they told her that she was to drive the English army out of France and bring the young French prince to be crowned king. She didn't know what to do, but by the time she was sixteen, she persuaded one of her relatives to bring her to the king. They turned her away at first, but she soon persuaded the king that she was God's messenger. She then dressed as a soldier and led the French army to defeat the British at a battle in Orléans. Later on, she was captured by the British, who accused her of heresy and being a witch. A Church court convicted her and she was burned at the stake. But a second trial overturned this, and she was eventually declared a saint. She is the patroness of France.

LORD JESUS,
you inspired St. Joan of Arc to believe that the vision
she had was true
and gave her the courage to follow your calling.
Help us to listen when you call us to help others
and give us the courage to tell the truth.
We thank you for this meal
and ask your blessing on people serving in the military.
Keep them safe and help them in their needs.
Amen.

May 31: The Visitation

We remember today how Mary, a very young woman in the first month of her pregnancy, went to visit her cousin Elizabeth, an old woman in her sixth month. Mary made a long and difficult journey from Nazareth to the hill country of Judea to be with her cousin, to offer her help and support, and to share with her the news that she had received from the angel Gabriel. When she arrived, Mary proclaimed the beautiful prayer we call the Magnificat.

OUR SOULS PROCLAIM YOUR GREATNESS, O GOD,
and our spirits rejoice in you, our Savior.
For you have done great things for us,
and holy is your name.
You turn away the proud and the selfish,
but you raise up the lowly and the poor.
Teach us to be grateful for all your gifts
and to follow Mary's example of thoughtfulness
to others.
Bless this meal, and make our lives holy,
through Jesus, the Son of Mary and our brother.
Amen.

Memorial Day

The Last Monday of May

On this day we remember all those who have died in the many wars fought by our nation. Since 1950, by the request of Congress, it is also a day to pray for peace. This day used to be called Decoration Day because of the custom of decorating the graves of soldiers, a practice that began after the American Civil War.

GOD OF PEACE,
we recall today the words of Jesus,
"Blessed are the peacemakers,
for they will be called children of God."
As we remember all who have died because of war,
we pray that their sacrifices may bring peace to
our world.
Inspire the leaders of all nations
to turn away from war and work for peace.
As we celebrate this day with our family and friends,
bless this food we share.
Help us to live in peace with one another,
and with people of every nation, race, and creed.
Amen.

June: The Most Sacred Heart of Jesus

The Friday after Trinity Sunday

Today we celebrate the Feast of the Sacred Heart of Jesus. We often think of our heart as the place where love comes from. When we celebrate Jesus' Sacred Heart, we celebrate his love for us. During his life, Jesus had great love for his family and friends. He especially showed his love for the sick and the poor. He said that the greatest love of all was to "lay down" your life for your friends. We do that whenever we think of others' needs ahead of our own.

DEAR JESUS,
we are very happy today to celebrate
how much you love us.
Your heart was full of love for all.
We ask you to also fill our hearts with love,
for our family and friends
and especially for those who are sick or poor.
Fill us with gratitude
for all you have given us
and for this good food that we now share.
Amen.

June: Immaculate Heart of Mary

The Saturday after the Feast of the Sacred Heart

The Gospel of Luke tells the story of how Jesus was separated from his parents on a return trip home from Jerusalem. They finally found him in the Temple, discussing the scriptures with the priests there. At the end, Luke tells us that Mary kept all of these things in her heart. Today we honor Mary and think about her loving heart. From the moment the angel Gabriel told her she would become the mother of the Savior, she said yes. We call her heart "immaculate" because she always gave her heart entirely to God. Her love for her son, Jesus, never failed. Her love for us never fails either, no matter how we act.

GOD, OUR FATHER,
you gave Mary a heart that was ready
to welcome your Son, Jesus.
Your Holy Spirit overshadowed her
and she treasured all that happened in her heart.
Give us hearts ready to receive your Son,
and through Mary's help
make us ready to welcome Jesus into our lives
and respond to whatever he calls us to do.
Give us hearts that are grateful for all your gifts,
especially this meal we now share.
Amen.

June 3: St. Charles Lwanga and Companions

When Catholic and Anglican missionaries first came to Uganda in 1879, they were welcomed by King Mutesa. Many members of the king's court became Catholics. But when the king died, his son Mwanga took the throne. He was a violent and corrupt man who was especially cruel to the boys in his court. When his chief assistant Joseph Mukasa condemned the king for killing an Anglican bishop and his companions, the king stabbed him with a spear and then had him killed. Charles Lwanga, just twenty-five years old, then took charge of protecting the young boys and educated them in the faith. But the king's anger soon flared again, and he had Charles and all of the boys tortured and put to death.

DEAR LORD,
we know that there is so much evil in the world
and that people with power sometimes use it to
harm others.
We thank you for the courage of these martyrs
from Uganda,
who stood up to evil and tried to protect the young.
We thank you for your presence with us as we share
this meal
and ask you to fill our hearts with courage and concern
to do what is right.
Amen.

June 12: Anne Frank

Not long after the Nazis invaded the Netherlands in 1940, they began to arrest Jewish people and send them to concentration camps. Anne Frank was thirteen when her family went into hiding in a secret part of their home. For more than two years, Anne, her sister Margot, and their parents lived with another family of three in just four rooms. Anne had received a diary for her thirteenth birthday and began to write about her life in hiding. *The Diary of Anne Frank* has become one of the most important accounts of the Holocaust—the persecution and killing of the Jews by the Nazis. It is still read today by many people, young and old. Anne's family was discovered on August 4, 1944. They were arrested and sent to concentration camps. Only Anne's father, Otto, survived.

BLESSED ARE YOU, GOD OF ALL PEOPLES.
You first revealed yourself to the Jews
and made an everlasting covenant with them.
Today we remember the suffering and death
of Anne Frank, her family, and the millions of Jews
who were killed in the Holocaust.
We ask you to help us recognize any prejudice in
our minds
and to show us how to respect and reverence people
of all faiths.
Be with us now as we share this food
and guide us to make this world a place
of peace and harmony among all.
Amen.

June 13: St. Anthony of Padua

Although he is greatly revered as an Italian saint, Anthony was actually born in Portugal in 1195. At the age of fifteen, he joined the Augustinians and became very learned, especially in the scriptures. At about the age of twenty-six, he joined the Franciscans and went to teach in Morocco. When returning, his ship was blown off course and he landed in Italy where he became a great preacher.

St. Anthony is often called upon to help find lost objects. Although no one is sure why, the story goes that a young novice once ran away with a valuable book of the psalms that Anthony was using. When Anthony prayed for its recovery, the young man had a frightening vision and brought it back.

God of love,
you called Anthony to preach the Good News
and gave him a love for the poor and the lost.
Fill us with enthusiasm for your Word,
and by this meal,
strengthen us to reach out
to the hungry, the lonely, and the sick.
We thank you for these and all your gifts in Jesus' name.
Amen.

First Day of Summer

GOD OF LIGHT AND LOVE,
we thank you for this season of summer,
a time of warmth, growth, and fun.
May the brightness of the sun remind us of your love.
May the coolness of the waters renew us in your care.
As we rejoice in this season,
help us to be grateful for all your gifts,
especially the food on our table.
Make us mindful, too, of those who are hungry,
and teach us how to care for them.
We ask this through Jesus,
our light and our Lord.
Amen.

June 22: St. Thomas More

King Henry VIII of England wanted to have a son to succeed him. During the twenty-five years of his marriage to Catherine, they had a number of children, but the only boy died as an infant. So, Henry decided to annul his marriage and marry someone else. When the pope refused to do this, Henry decided that the Church of England would break away from the rest of the Church and he would be the head of it instead of the pope. Thomas More was a close advisor and friend of the king and was widely respected by the people. But when he refused to accept what Henry was doing, the king imprisoned him in the Tower of London. He was eventually put on trial for treason and convicted. He was beheaded in 1535. At his execution he said that he would die "the king's good servant, but God's first."

WE THANK YOU, LORD, FOR THE EXAMPLE OF
ST. THOMAS MORE,
who stood up against the wrongdoing of the king.
Give us the courage we need
to be true to what is right
and not to give in to fear
about what others might say.
Bless this food we share.
May it strengthen us always
to do what is right and just.
Amen.

Father's Day

The Third Sunday in June

O GOD, OUR FATHER,
we thank you for giving us Dad
and for the many ways he shows us your fatherly care.
On this his special day,
we ask you to bless him with your peace and joy.
Give him the strength and the understanding
that he needs to care for us as a family.
Help us to appreciate more all that he does for us
and to show him how much we love him.
Bless this meal that we share to celebrate Dad,
and be with all fathers and grandfathers on this day.
Amen.

June 24: The Birth of St. John the Baptist

Although we do not know the actual day of John's birth, St. Luke's gospel tells us that after the annunciation, Mary went to visit Elizabeth, John's mother, who was in her sixth month of pregnancy. Since the annunciation is celebrated on March 25, John's birthday comes three months later, on June 24.

This day is almost six months opposite from Christmas and very close to the first day of summer. Just as John once said of Jesus, "He must increase; I must decrease" (Jn 3:30), Christians have noted how after the birthday of John the Baptist, the days begin to grow shorter, while after Jesus' birthday they get longer.

God of our ancestors,
you called John while still in his mother's womb
to announce the coming of Jesus.
As we begin this season of summer,
make us aware of the many chances ahead of us
to be signs of your love.
We thank you for this meal
and for the opportunity it gives us
to serve and care for one another.
Amen.

June 27: Helen Keller

Helen Keller was born in Tuscumbia, Alabama, on this date in 1880. Due to a severe illness at the age of nineteen months, she became blind and deaf. A short time later, she lost her ability to speak. When she was almost seven years old her parents found a wonderful teacher for her. With Anne Mansfield Sullivan's help, Helen began to speak after just one month. Eventually she learned to read Braille and to write as well. Helen attended school and eventually went to college. She wrote many books about her life and her struggle to achieve, despite her disabilities.

DEAR GOD,
thank you for the gifts of sight, hearing, and speech.
Help us not to take them for granted
and to use all the gifts you give us to help others.
And help us also to remember
that when bodies are not so agile
or minds are not so quick,
that each of us nevertheless has special gifts
to share with one another.
We give you thanks for the gift of this food
and for all the talents and abilities we have received
through your generous love.
Amen.

June 29: Sts. Peter and Paul

It is an ancient tradition to celebrate these two apostles' feasts together. Although their lives were quite different, there are many parallels between them. Both were great leaders in the Early Church: Peter as the leader of the apostles, and Paul as a great missionary. Both were given new names by Jesus as signs of their new missions. Jesus changed Simon's name to Peter, meaning "rock" and Saul's name to Paul to signify his new mission to the Gentiles. Both were eventually put to death in Rome for their faith.

LORD JESUS,
you called Peter and Paul
to share their faith and love for you with the
 whole world.
You gave them new names and led them to do things
beyond what they could ever have imagined.
Just as you strengthened them by your presence
at table and the Eucharist,
be with us during this meal
to renew our faith and love.
Help us, like Peter, to put our faith in you;
and like Paul, to make love our greatest gift.
Bless this food and the friendship we share.
Amen.

July 1: St. Junípero Serra

Known as the apostle of California, Junípero Serra was a Franciscan priest from the island of Majorca, Spain. He came to Mexico in 1750, where he worked with native peoples for eighteen years. When he was fifty-four years old, he began to work in California, and after one year he founded the San Diego Mission in 1769. Over the next fifteen years he built eight more missions in California. Many of these have become major cities, such as Los Angeles and San Francisco. In thirty-five years as a missionary, he is said to have walked ten thousand miles. He died on August 28, 1784, at Carmel, California, and was canonized a saint by Pope Francis in 2015.

DEAR GOD,
you gave Junípero Serra the courage and faith
to spread the Good News
among the people of Mexico and California.
We thank you for the gift of faith
and we ask you for the courage to follow your call
to us.
As you cared for Junípero on his many journeys,
let your love guide us everywhere we go.
We thank you for this food before us.
Bless it and bless us with your presence.
Amen.

July 3: St. Thomas the Apostle

Thomas was one of Jesus' twelve apostles. The first time he speaks in St. John's gospel is when Jesus is about to go to Bethany where Lazarus has just died. People there had once tried to stone Jesus, and the other apostles were telling him not to go back. But Thomas said, "Let us also go to die with him" (Jn 11:16). He is often called "Doubting Thomas" because when Jesus appeared to his disciples after the Resurrection, Thomas was not there. When they told him about it, he said he would not believe until he could see for himself and even put his hand into the wound in Jesus' side. A week later, Jesus appeared to the disciples again and this time Thomas was there. Jesus invited him to touch his wounds and believe. Then Thomas said, "My Lord and my God!" (Jn 20:24–29).

LORD JESUS,
you gave Thomas a bold spirit to say what he
    was thinking.
He was your true friend even though he doubted.
Thank you for calling us to be your friends
and showing us your love even when we doubt you.
You call us to touch your wounds
when we act kindly to those who are hurting.
Help us to see you in one another as we share this
    meal together.
Amen.

July 4: Independence Day

On July 4, 1776, the Continental Congress issued the Declaration of Independence. Written mostly by Thomas Jefferson, it declared the Thirteen Colonies to be free and independent states, no longer subject to the king of England. Although the Revolutionary War had already begun, this was the official birth of the United States.

O God, our Creator,
with the founders of our country
we believe that you have given all people
"certain inalienable rights . . . among these, life, liberty, and the pursuit of happiness."
We thank you for our country—
for the freedom and opportunity it gives us,
and for its beauty and bounty.
As we celebrate with this meal,
we ask you to bless our food and our nation.
Give us leaders inspired by its ideals
and mindful of the rights of all people.
Help us to use our gifts wisely
and to extend your care to the needy of the world.
We ask this through Christ, our Lord.
Amen.

July 5: Bl. Pier Giorgio Frassati

Pier Giorgio Frassati was born in 1901. His father owned a newspaper and his mother was a well-known painter. Although his family was not religious, Giorgio was very devoted to attending Mass and praying before the Blessed Sacrament. He loved to climb mountains, and he was also known for playing jokes on his friends. But Giorgio is best known for his love for the poor. He often gave away his money and even his clothing to people he met on the street. He would say, "Charity is not enough; we need social reform." When he was just twenty-four, he developed polio. He died on July 4, 1925, only five days after he became ill. His parents expected only his friends and their associates to attend the funeral, but they were shocked to see thousands of the poor lining the streets to honor him.

Lord Jesus,
you gave Pier Giorgio Frassati a deep devotion
to your presence in the Eucharist and your presence in the poor.
His enthusiasm brought joy to his friends,
and his generosity provided comfort for the poor.
Give us that same love for you through the Eucharist,
in one another, in our friends,
and in the poor and suffering people we meet.
We thank you for the gift of this meal
and all the gifts we have from your goodness.
Amen.

July 11: Sts. Benedict and Scholastica

Benedict and Scholastica were not only brother and sister but also twins! They were born to wealthy parents and had many choices before them. Benedict studied in Rome but became disillusioned with the greed and fighting he experienced there. He decided to dedicate his life to God. First he lived as a hermit, but then others joined him and he started the first monastery. Monks lived together with the motto Pray and Work.

Like her brother, Scholastica also dedicated her life to God and started the first community of women. Her monastery was just five miles away from Benedict's, and once a year they would spend a day together at a farmhouse. Benedictine monks and sisters became the largest group of religious in Europe. They were especially dedicated to offering hospitality to strangers.

LORD JESUS,
help us to follow the example of
saints Benedict and Scholastica.
They helped each other to grow in love for you
and invited many others to join them.
Help us to continue to grow closer as a family.
May we make our home a place of welcome to all
as a sign of our gratitude to you for all the wonderful
things we enjoy,
Amen.

July 12: Sts. Louis and Zélie Martin

Louis Martin and Zélie Guérin were married on July 12, 1858, in the small French town of Alençon. Louis, thirty-four, was a watchmaker, and Zélie, twenty-six, had her own business making lace. Earlier in his life, Louis wanted to be a monk, but he was rejected because he couldn't learn Latin. Zélie had tried to become a nun, but she, too, was turned away because of poor health. Louis and Zélie had nine children—seven girls and two boys. Sadly, though, both of the boys and two of the girls died from illnesses at very young ages. Zélie once wrote about her family, "We lived only for them, they were all our happiness." Their last child was also very sickly, and Zélie doubted that she would survive past infancy. But this baby girl lived and brought much joy to her family. Her name was Thérèse. She became a nun, as did all of her sisters. Today we know her as St. Thérèse of Lisieux. Zélie and Louis had a strong faith that helped them survive the sadness of losing four of their children. They passed that faith on to their daughters. On October 19, 2008, they were the first married couple to be made saints together.

Dear God, you gave Louis and Zélie a deep love for you
that they shared with their children
to help them grow in faith and devotion to you.
Give our family the same love for one another
to help us grow closer to you.
We thank you for your presence in our family
and ask you to bless this meal that we share.
Amen.

July 13: St. Veronica

The Stations of the Cross are a devotion or prayer practice that helps us remember Jesus' walk to Calvary where he died on the Cross. At the sixth station we remember how Veronica wiped the face of Jesus with a towel and the blood-stained image of his face was preserved on it. All we know about Veronica is this one moment in her life. Moved with love and compassion for Jesus, she bravely stepped forward to offer him this tender act of kindness.

DEAR JESUS,
we remember how you loved us and suffered so much
for our sakes.
Give us hearts full of compassion and courage
like Veronica's
to recognize your face in the suffering of others—
especially the poor, the sick, or the lonely—
and to do what we can to comfort and help them.
Please bless this meal and keep us always in your care.
Amen.

July 14: St. Kateri Tekakwitha

Tekakwitha was born around 1756 in a small village in central New York. Her father was a Mohawk chief. Her mother was a member of the Algonquin tribe. When she was about four years old, her parents and her brother died in a smallpox epidemic. She survived, but she had terrible scars on her face and poor eyesight. Tekakwitha was then adopted by her father's brother. One day, three Jesuit missionaries came to her village. Tekakwitha was very moved by their preaching. She refused to marry the man her uncle had chosen for her and instead was baptized, taking the name Kateri, the Mohawk version of Catherine. She was rejected by the tribe and, on the advice of a priest, made a two-hundred-mile journey to a Christian village in Canada. Kateri died at the young age of twenty-four and is the first Native American person to be named a saint.

DEAR JESUS,
when St. Kateri Tekakwitha lost her parents and was made fun of by others
because of her scars and poor eyesight,
she found comfort and strength in friendship with you.
We thank you for her example and ask you to keep us close to you
when we feel alone or rejected by others.
Thank you for this meal.
May we be grateful for all that we have.
Amen.

July 16: Our Lady of Mt. Carmel

Mt. Carmel is located on the coast of Israel, just north of the city of Haifa. Tradition holds that it was the place where the prophet Elijah confronted the pagan prophets of Baal (see 1 Kgs 18:19–46). It is an ancient shrine of Mary, and it was there that the Order of Our Lady of Mt. Carmel (or the Carmelites) was founded in about 1154. Our Lady of Mt. Carmel is especially honored by Italian Americans, who celebrate this day with festivals.

GOD OF THE MOUNTAINS AND VALLEYS,
you invite us to see you in the beauty of nature
and in the warmth of one another's love.
Help us to follow Mary and all the saints of Carmel
who sought your face in the silence of prayer.
Be with us on the mountaintops of joy
and in the valleys of sadness.
Give us an awareness of your presence in whatever
we do.
Fill us with gratitude for all your gifts,
especially for this meal that we share in your name.
Amen.

July 22: St. Mary Magdalene

Before she met Jesus, Mary Magdalene was known as a terrible sinner, but after her conversion she became one of his most dedicated followers. At the Crucifixion, most of the apostles ran away, but Mary was one of a few women who stood faithfully at the foot of Jesus' Cross. She was also one of the three women who came to anoint his body on Easter morning and discovered the empty tomb. As she stood weeping outside the tomb, she saw a man she thought was a gardener. When she asked where they had taken the body of Jesus, the man spoke her name. She recognized that he was indeed Jesus.

FAITHFUL GOD,
you transformed the life of Mary Magdalene by her
love of Jesus.
You gave her the courage
to abandon her old way of life to follow him,
and the devotion to stand by him
through the agony of the Cross.
You chose her as the first witness of Jesus' Resurrection
and sent her to proclaim the Good News.
Help us to imitate her and to grow in love for Jesus.
Through this meal that we share in Jesus' name,
help us to recognize Christ in one another
and fill us with the joy of his presence.
Amen.

July 25: St. James

James and his brother John were fishermen. When Jesus called them, they left their father's boat and followed him. Along with John and Peter, James was one of Jesus' closest friends. Jesus took them with him when he went to the top of Mt. Tabor and was transfigured. His clothes became dazzling white, and they heard God the Father speak, "This is my beloved Son, with whom I am well pleased; listen to him" (Mt 17:5). But James had his faults too. One time he asked Jesus to call down fire on some people who wouldn't believe in him. Another time, he wanted Jesus to give him and John the highest place in heaven. This made the other apostles angry. After the Resurrection, James became the leader of the Church in Jerusalem and was eventually put to death by King Herod. He was the first apostle to die for Jesus.

DEAR JESUS,
you call us your friends and ask us to follow you as St. James did.
Like him, we are not perfect.
We sometimes do mean things when we are angry
and can be selfish and think we are better than others,
but your love and friendship never fail.
Be with us as a family as we share this meal
and help us to be patient and tolerant with one another.
Amen.

July 26: Sts. Joachim and Ann

Although we do not know anything about their lives, and we cannot even be certain of their names, we remember Joachim and Ann as the parents of Mary. From what we know of their daughter, we can assume that they, too, were holy people. They, along with Joseph's parents, would have arranged their daughter's wedding; and Mary would have been living in their home at the time of the annunciation. We can only guess about their reaction to this news, as well as what role they played in the raising of their grandson, Jesus.

GENTLE GOD,
we thank you for the gift of parents and grandparents
who love and care for us throughout our lives.
As we remember Joachim and Ann,
the parents of Mary and the grandparents of Jesus,
we ask you to help us appreciate
all that we have received from our families.
As you were present at their table,
be here with us.
Nourish us with your grace
and fill us with compassion for all those in need.
Amen.

July 29: St. Martha

Martha lived with her sister Mary and her brother Lazarus in the village of Bethany, a short distance from Jerusalem. Jesus often stayed at their home, and one time, Martha complained to Jesus that Mary spent too much time talking with Jesus and not enough time working. Jesus told her that Mary had made the better choice. When their brother Lazarus died, it took Jesus four days to get there. When Martha heard that Jesus was near, she ran out to meet him and said, "Lord, if you had been here, my brother would not have died" (Jn 11:21). In response to her faith, Jesus raised Lazarus back to life.

LORD JESUS,
we remember today that you shared many meals
with your friends Martha, Mary, and Lazarus.
You laughed and cried with them.
You settled their arguments and took away
  their sorrow.
May your quiet presence at our table
bring us the same happiness and peace.
Bless our food and be with us always,
in times of trouble and in times of joy.
Amen.

July 31: St. Ignatius of Loyola

Ignatius was born in the village of Loyola in the Basque region of Spain in 1491. His mother died shortly after his birth and he was raised by the local blacksmith's wife. Growing up, he loved to read about the heroism of soldiers in battle. He joined the army, but when he was thirty years old his leg was shattered by a cannonball. While recovering in the hospital, where there were no books about the military, he began to read the Bible and books about the lives of the saints. Soon he realized that there was something greater than being a soldier, and he devoted himself to a new mission, following Jesus. Ignatius founded the Society of Jesus (Jesuits), a community that continues his work of education and service to the Church today.

LORD JESUS,
when St. Ignatius was badly injured in battle,
you gently guided him to give up his dreams of glory
and dedicate himself to serving you as a teacher and
 spiritual guide.
Help us to think about how we can serve you
in whatever dreams we have for the future.
As we gather at this table, help us to encourage
 one another
in our daily tasks and recognize that you are here
 with us,
just as you are present in everything we do.
Amen.

August 1: St. Alphonsus Liguori

Alphonsus was the oldest of eight children. His father was a captain in the navy, and from a young age Alphonsus was expected to follow in his footsteps. But Alphonsus had very poor eyesight, and he was also very short. So instead of the navy, he studied law. He was very smart, and by the age of sixteen he had already finished his studies and he became a lawyer. Although he was very successful, he wasn't really happy being a lawyer. After he lost a big case, he reconsidered what he was doing. He felt that God was calling him to become a priest, and so he gave up the law and went to the seminary. As a priest he worked with the poor and was a very good preacher. He always wanted people to know that God is not a severe judge but a merciful and loving Father.

LOVING FATHER,
you gave St. Alphonsus Liguori
the gift of great intelligence and a heart full
of compassion
for people who were struggling.
Help us to use our minds to understand other
people better
and to care about their needs and worries.
Help us especially to show your love
and understanding
to one another in our family as we share this meal,
for which we give you thanks.
Amen.

August 4: St. John Vianney

For the first thirteen years of John Vianney's life, it was against the law to go to Mass. It was the time of the French Revolution, and John's family would travel a long way from their farm to go to secret Masses. The priests were on the run and John looked up to them as heroes. He wanted to become a priest, too, but when he was old enough, he was drafted into the army two times. The first time he got sick, the second, the troops left without him. He had to hide out because if he was found he would be arrested as a deserter. When the war ended, he was able to go to the seminary. But John was not a very good student, and he almost flunked out. Once he finally became a priest, he was sent to a small remote village where he spent the rest of his life. Fr. John was compassionate and a very good listener. He spent many hours each day counseling people in the Sacrament of Penance. People came from many miles away and would wait in line for hours to go to Confession with him.

Dear Jesus,
you called St. John Vianney to be a priest
and gave him tremendous compassion and patience.
We thank you for the Sacrament of Penance
and for your compassion and patience with us when we have sinned.
Help us to forgive one another and to be patient with one another.
Bless this food that we have to eat
through your generous love for us.
Amen.

August 6: The Transfiguration

Today we remember how Jesus took Peter, James, and John to the top of a mountain. There, as the Gospel of Matthew tells us, "his face shone like the sun and his clothes became white as light" (17:2). Moses and Elijah appeared with him. Although Peter was frightened, he said, "Lord, it is good that we are here," and offered to build three shelters (17:4). Just then the voice of God was heard, "This is my beloved Son . . . listen to him" (Mt 17:5).

HOLY GOD,
you gave us your Son, Jesus,
to show us your love and to guide us to you.
We thank you for the times when we have seen his face
in one another, in our friends,
in those who are hungry, and in those who are sad.
As we gather around this table, we say with Peter,
"Lord, it is good that we are here."
Bless our food and our conversation.
Teach us to listen to one another
and help us always to listen to you.
We ask this in Jesus' name.
Amen.

August 8: St. Dominic

Dominic grew up in a noble family and was a very bright and hardworking student. He owned many books and valuable manuscripts. But when he was twenty-one there was a famine in Spain. He sold his books and manuscripts and even his clothes to buy food for the hungry. Then he became a monk. He traveled to Rome to ask the pope to send him to distant lands. But the pope asked him to go to France and convince a group of Christians who had left the Church to come back. Because he was such a good preacher who lived a simple life, people listened to him. Soon others joined him and formed the Order of Preachers. Today they are known as Dominicans—priests and sisters who serve the poor, teach in schools, and preach the Gospel all over the world.

Dear Lord,
you gave St. Dominic the gifts of compassion
and generosity,
even to sell his prized possessions and buy food for
the hungry.
Help us not to be selfish with things that are special
to us,
but instead generous when people ask us to share.
We thank you for this good food before us.
May our time together at this meal
help us to be more compassionate and generous
with others.
Amen.

August 9: St. Teresa Benedicta of the Cross

Before she became a nun, St. Teresa Benedicta's name was Edith Stein. She grew up in a devoted Jewish family, but when she was a teenager she stopped believing in God. Edith studied at an important university in Germany and became a philosopher. After completing her studies, she read the autobiography of St. Teresa of Ávila. This convinced her to believe in God again and to become a Catholic. Eventually she became a nun. When the Nazis began to arrest and persecute the Jews, she spoke out against them. Her order transferred her to the Netherlands, so she would be safe from arrest. But after a few more years, the Nazis took over the Netherlands and she was arrested. She was sent to Auschwitz, a concentration camp, where she was put to death on this date in 1942.

Dear God,
even though young Edith stopped believing in you,
you never abandoned her.
Through her studies and the example of St. Teresa of Ávila
you led her to believe in you again.
Be with us on our life journeys
and give us the courage she showed to speak out against evil and hatred.
As we gather to share this meal,
help us to remember that all that we have comes from you.
Amen.

August 11: St. Clare of Assisi

Clare was born in the Italian town of Assisi in 1194, thirteen years after St. Francis. As a teenager, she heard Francis preach and felt called to become one of his followers. At the age of eighteen, when her wealthy family wanted her to marry, she ran away to follow Francis. After a few years she became the leader of the first community of Franciscan sisters at San Damiano. There she lived a life of prayer and community and was a great help to Francis. She died in 1253.

GRACIOUS GOD,
you filled St. Clare with so much love
that she longed to spend her life
in prayer and service to others.
You gave her the courage to leave behind
a life of comfort and security
for an unknown and uncertain future.
Fill us with the same love for you and for others.
As you gave Clare and Francis the gift of friendship,
give us friends to support and guide us.
Bless this food, bless us, and bless all of our friends.
Amen.

August 12: St. Philomena

All that we know for sure about St. Philomena is that she died as a martyr. In the catacombs (underground tunnels in Rome), three tiles were found on a burial chamber with the words "Peace be with you, Philomena" in Latin. Through the centuries, pilgrims traveled to the church where her bones were and miracles of healing occurred there. According to a vision given to Sr. Maria Luisa di Gesù almost two hundred years ago, Philomena promised Jesus that she would never marry. Instead, she would devote her life entirely to him. But Diocletian, the emperor of Rome, fell in love with her and wanted to marry her. When she refused, he ordered her put to death. First he whipped her, then he had an anchor tied to her and threw her into the sea, and then he had her shot with arrows. But each time God sent his angels to rescue her. Finally he had her beheaded. Although we can't be sure that these things all happened, Philomena did die as a martyr and these stories remind us of God's care and protection.

FATHER, YOU CHOSE ST. PHILOMENA TO BE YOUR
LOVING CHILD
and were with her through all of her sufferings.
And when she died, you gave her new life with you.
Help us to imitate her devotion to Jesus
and remain faithful to you even when it is difficult.
We thank you for this meal and for the joy of believing
in you.
Amen.

August 14: St. Maximilian Kolbe

Maximilian Kolbe was born in Poland in 1894. His father was a weaver, and his mother was a midwife. From a young age he was very devoted to the Blessed Mother. He joined the Franciscans and was sent to study in Rome. He was a teacher, he opened a publishing house, and he even started a radio station. He also was a missionary in China, Japan, and India. But because of illness he had to return to Poland. When World War II started and the Nazis were persecuting the Jews, he hid two thousand people from them. But eventually the Nazis found out and sent him to Auschwitz, a concentration camp. When one of the prisoners escaped, the warden said ten men would have to die. One of the men chosen cried out, "My wife, my children!" St. Maximilian volunteered to take his place. He was killed on this date in 1942.

LORD JESUS,
you said there is no greater love
than to lay down your life for a friend.
Thank you for the courage and selflessness of St.
Maximilian Kolbe.
Help us to be courageous and selfless
when we see someone being treated badly.
We give you thanks for this food.
Through the love of your mother, Mary,
give us the generosity to share what we have
with others.
Amen.

August 15: The Assumption

Although we do not know anything about Mary's life after the day of Pentecost, Christian tradition holds that Mary spent the last years of her life with the apostle John in Ephesus, a town in present-day Turkey. However, there is also a church in Jerusalem located at the legendary place of her death called the Church of the Dormition (which means "falling asleep").

Since the seventh century, Christians have celebrated the Assumption. This celebration is based on the belief that Mary was taken up into heaven "body and soul." She now enjoys the fullness of salvation that we will all share in the resurrection of the dead.

EVER-LIVING GOD,
you called Mary to be the mother of your Son, Jesus.
When her life of service and witness was through,
you gave her the fullness of joy in heaven.
As we remember her faith and generous love,
help us to follow her example.
As we share this meal, we look forward to the day
when we will celebrate
a great and joyful banquet at your table in heaven
with Mary, with all the saints, and with all those
we love.
Amen.

August 22: The Queenship of Mary

One week ago, we celebrated the Assumption of Mary, body and soul, into heaven. Today we celebrate her as the Queen of Heaven and the queen of our hearts. Since early Christian times, Mary has been celebrated in hymns and art under this title. The name Regina, meaning "queen," is given to girls in honor of Mary.

> HAIL HOLY QUEEN,
> Mother of Mercy,
> our life, our sweetness, our hope!
> We praise you for the selfless love
> you showed as the mother of Jesus,
> and we thank you for your tender care for us.
> Lead us always to Jesus
> and help us to live as his friends and followers.
> We thank you, Lord, for the love of your mother.
> Bless this food and keep us always close to her.
> Amen.

August 24: St. Bartholomew

Bartholomew was one of the apostles. In the Gospels of Matthew, Mark, and Luke, he is always mentioned along with Philip, so perhaps they were friends. In St. John's gospel, Philip goes to tell Nathanael about Jesus. Since Bartholomew is not mentioned in John's gospel, many think that Nathanael and Bartholomew are two names for the same person. Jesus said that Nathanael was "a true Israelite. There is no duplicity in him" (Jn 1:47). He meant that Nathanael was always honest and truthful. Bartholomew was present when Jesus ascended to heaven and he followed the Lord's command to go forth and spread the Gospel. He traveled to Armenia and perhaps even to India. Like all the apostles except John, he was martyred for his preaching.

DEAR JESUS,
you called St. Bartholomew and his friend St. Philip
to be your apostles and friends.
You praised him for his truthfulness
and were always with him as he preached the Gospel.
We thank you for your friendship to us and for all the friends we have.
Help us to be honest and truthful when we speak
and keep us always close to you.
Bless this meal that we share and make us grateful for all we have.
Amen.

August 27 and 28: Sts. Monica and Augustine

St. Monica and St. Augustine are unique among the saints remembered through the year because they are mother and son. They came from the city of Tagaste in North Africa. As a brilliant young man, Augustine pursued his goal of becoming a teacher. He lived a wild life, caring little for anything but his own pleasure. For a while, Monica would not even let him enter her house, but then she had a vision that he would be converted. She prayed for him constantly and even followed him all the way to Milan, Italy. There Augustine experienced an unexpected conversion to Christ. He went on to become a great leader and teacher in the Early Church. Monica died shortly after her son's conversion.

FAITHFUL GOD,
you never give up on us,
even when we wander far from you.
Like a devoted mother, you are always there,
always ready to welcome us home.
As we remember the lives of St. Monica and
St. Augustine,
help us to open our hearts more widely to you
and fill us with gratitude
for these gifts of food and drink
and all of your many gifts.
Amen.

Labor Day

The First Monday in September

The first Labor Day took place in 1882 in New York City. The practice of a holiday to celebrate workers spread rapidly throughout the United States, and in 1894 President Grover Cleveland made this a national holiday. Today, Labor Day also marks the end of the summer vacation season.

HOLY GOD,
your grace is always at work in our lives.
You labored for six days to create the world,
and then you rested.
You sent your Son, Jesus, among us
to work as a carpenter and to preach the Good News.
Your Spirit is always active in the world,
recreating and renewing it with your love.
We thank you for this day to celebrate our work.
We are grateful for the strength of our bodies,
the skills of our hands, and the knowledge of
our minds.
We remember also those who are unemployed
or disabled.
Strengthen and guide them.
Thank you for this meal
and all who labored so that we might enjoy it.
Amen.

September 5: St. Teresa of Calcutta

Known around the world as Mother Teresa, St. Teresa of Calcutta was actually born not in India but in Skopje, Macedonia, in 1910. As a child, she loved stories of missionaries in India, and at eighteen she joined the Sisters of Loreto. The following year she began her life in India where she taught in a school in Calcutta. Although she loved teaching, she was terribly disturbed by the desperate poverty all around her. One day while traveling on a train, she felt God calling her to begin a new ministry with the poor. Many people in Calcutta were dying in the street because there was no one to care for them. Mother Teresa lived in the slums and established a home for the dying. She and other sisters would bring them in and care for them. Her ministry grew, and she founded an order called the Missionaries of Charity. She eventually won the Nobel Peace Prize for her work. She died in 1997 and was made a saint in 2015.

LORD JESUS,
thank you for the inspiring life of St. Teresa of Calcutta.
Help us to follow her example by caring for the poor
and to put into practice these words of hers:
"Not all of us can do great things.
But we can do small things with great love."
Help us to do small things with great love.
Thank you for this food. Let it strengthen us
to grow in love and compassion.
Amen.

September 8: The Birth of Mary

Although we do not know the date of Mary's birth, Christians have celebrated it on this day since the seventh century. The date of the Feast of the Immaculate Conception, December 8, was determined by counting back nine months from this date, the time from conception to birth. Mary's birthday is one of only three birthdays celebrated in the Christian calendar. Along with the birth of Jesus and John the Baptist, it celebrates the dawn of salvation.

God of life and love,
we celebrate today the birth of Mary.
From the first moment of her life, you called her
by name
and prepared her for the great work
she was to do as the mother of Jesus.
Help us to hear your call each day
and to say yes when you ask us to serve you.
As we share this meal together, help us to be grateful
for all the opportunities you give us as a family
to care for one another and to reach out to those
in need.
Bless this food and bless us all in Jesus' name.
Amen.

September 9: St. Peter Claver

As a young Jesuit, Peter Claver was sent from his home in Spain to Cartagena, a port city in Columbia. Every year, ten thousand slaves were brought to Cartagena from Africa. The conditions on the ships were so terrible that about one-third of them died on the way. As soon as a ship arrived, Peter would go on board with food and medicine for the prisoners. Once they were on land and locked up in pens, he would visit them often. In addition to providing for their many needs, he used pictures and the help of translators to tell them about Jesus and God's love for them. He worked among the slaves for forty years and baptized them, perhaps as many as three hundred thousand! He died in 1654, alone and forgotten by the authorities. But when the ordinary people heard of his death, they came in great numbers and a huge funeral was held to remember what he did.

LORD JESUS,
you gave St. Peter Claver the courage and compassion
to go out to the slave ships that were filled with disease
and filth.
He recognized the slaves as his brothers and sisters
and lovingly cared for them.
Help us to see those whom the world hates and rejects
as our brothers and sisters
and to learn how we can better care for them.
Thank you for this meal and for all that we have.
Amen.

September 11: 9/11

On this day in 2001, the terrorist group al-Qaeda coordinated an attack on the United States. Four planes were hijacked. Two were crashed into the World Trade Center complex, the Twin Towers, the largest buildings in New York City, causing them to collapse. One hit the Pentagon in Arlington, Virginia. The fourth crashed in a field in Shanksville, Pennsylvania, when the passengers fought the hijackers and prevented them from hitting their target, thought to be the White House. Almost three thousand people died that day and more than six thousand were injured. Each year on this day we pause to remember the victims of these attacks as well as the many who died in the wars that followed.

O GOD OF MERCY AND JUSTICE,
we pray for an end to hatred and the violence that
it brings.
Help us to seek peace, not revenge.
We remember the innocent and heroic people
who died on 9/11
as well as their families and friends.
Keep them always in your care
and bless this meal we share today.
Amen.

September 15: Our Lady of Sorrows

Despite the deep and lasting joy of being the mother of the Lord, Mary experienced many sorrows during her life. Today's feast day reminds us of that. The popular devotion called the Seven Sorrows of Mary focuses on these painful moments in her life:

1. The prophecy of Simeon that a sword would pierce Mary's heart (Lk 2:25–35)
2. The flight into Egypt (Mt 2:13–15)
3. Loss of the child Jesus for three days (Lk 2:41–50)
4. Mary meets Jesus on his way to Calvary (Lk 23:27–31)
5. Crucifixion and death of Jesus (Jn 19:25–30)
6. The body of Jesus being taken from the Cross (Jn 19:31–37)
7. The burial of Jesus (Lk 23:50–56)

Dear Mary,
help us to have hearts like yours,
filled with compassion for all the suffering in
this world.
Through your Son, Jesus, make us aware of the pain
and suffering
among people in our family, friends, and neighbors.
And give us a sense of gratitude for all we have.
Amen.

September 20: Sts. Andrew Kim Taegon, Paul Chong Hasang, and Companions

Today we celebrate the memory of two saints who stand for the tens of thousands of Catholics who were martyrs for their faith in Korea. Christianity came to Korea in the late 1700s, when a number of Korean scholars obtained books about Christianity through the Korean embassy in China. When the first priest came to Korea from China in 1794, there were already more than four thousand Catholics there. The Church had grown even without priests and the sacraments because of the great faith of the people. However, the rulers of Korea did not like the Gospel's message of equality among all the children of God, and they persecuted the Church. Andrew Kim Taegon was the first Korean to be ordained a priest. But just one year later he was arrested, tortured, and put to death. His father, too, had been martyred seven years earlier, along with Paul Chong Hasang, a married lay apostle. Many others died for their faith in these years, including many women and young people.

GOD OF ALL NATIONS,
thank you for the example of faith and courage
in St. Andrew Kim Taegon, St. Paul Chong Hasang,
and all of the thousands of brave people
who founded the Church in Korea.
We pray for the Church in Korea today
and thank you for the many faithful Korean Catholics
in our country.
We thank you, too, for the gift of faith
and for this good food that we share.
Please help our faith to grow stronger
and keep us always in your care.
Amen.

만민의 주님이신 하느님,

성 김대건 안드레아 사제와 성 정하상 바오로와 한국 교회의 기초를 놓은 모든 수천명의 모든 용감한 신앙인들을 통해 보여주신 신앙과 용기의 본보기를 보여주심에 감사드리나이다.

오늘 저희는 한국 교회를 위하여 기도드리며 우리 나라에 많은 한국 천주교 신자들을 주심에 감사드리나이다.

또한 신앙의 선물과 우리가 나누고 있는 이 천상 양식을 주심에 감사드리나이다.

저희의 신앙이 더욱 굳건해질 수 있도록 도와주시고

언제나 저희를 보호하소서.

아멘.

September 21: St. Matthew

Matthew was a tax collector, and because of this he was hated by his fellow Jews. He worked for the Romans, not only collecting taxes for this occupying force but also keeping some for himself. Nevertheless, when Jesus passed by his tax office one day, he said, "Follow me" (Mt 9:9). Immediately Matthew got up and followed him. Matthew then gave a dinner for Jesus, inviting other tax collectors and notorious sinners. When the Pharisees complained about this, Jesus said, "Those who are healthy do not need a physician, but the sick do" (Lk 5:31). Matthew became one of Jesus' followers and eventually composed the gospel that bears his name.

God of mercy,
you sent us Jesus to proclaim your love
for the rich and poor, for the good and bad.
Help us to hear his call
and, like Matthew, to follow him.
May we always welcome Jesus to our table
and recognize his presence
in the faces of those whom others despise.
Bless this food and teach us to share
your blessings with others.
Amen.

September 23: Padre Pio

Francesco Forgione was born in the small Italian village of Pietrelcina on May 25, 1887. He grew up on his family's small farm where he tended sheep. At the age of fifteen, he became a friar and took the name Pio. Despite poor health, he completed his studies and became a priest. During World War I, he served in the medical core. One day soon after this, Padre Pio had a vision of Jesus. When the vision ended, he had the stigmata—the wounds of Jesus on his hands, feet, and side were miraculously on Padre Pio's body as well. As this became known, many people came to him for Confession and to pray for healing. He was very compassionate toward them all and spent the rest of his life hearing confessions and ministering to the sick. Padre Pio's motto was "Pray, hope, and don't worry." On June 16, 2002, he was made a saint—officially known as St. Pius of Pietrelcina—by Pope John Paul II.

DEAR JESUS,
you gave Padre Pio the strength to share in your
very wounds,
and from his suffering he learned to
care compassionately
for all who came to him.
Help our family when we suffer and give us the grace
to pray, hope, and not worry.
Thank you for this meal and all we receive through
your grace.
Amen.

First Day of Autumn

BOUNTIFUL GOD,
as the season of fall begins, we are grateful
for the rich harvest of the earth:
for corn and wheat,
for apples and peaches,
for fish and fowl.
As the days grow shorter
and the nights turn colder,
we rely on your love to warm us and sustain us.
As we are grateful for your gifts,
make us mindful of others
and generous with what we have.
Bless this meal that we share in the name of Jesus,
our Lord.
Amen.

September 27: St. Vincent de Paul

Vincent de Paul grew up on a small farm near Toulouse, France. When he was sixteen, his father sold the family's oxen to pay for him to go to the seminary. Vincent was a very bright student, but at first his motive for becoming a priest was to have a comfortable life and provide for his family. But his life changed when as a young priest he was kidnapped by pirates and sold into slavery. After two years he was finally able to return to France, where he became chaplain to a noble family. He was put in charge of giving money to the poor. From then on, he dedicated himself to caring for the poor, the sick, and convicts, and also to preaching about the work of charity. He began a religious order for men that today is named after him, the Vincentians. With St. Louise de Marillac he founded a women's community called the Daughters of Charity.

LORD JESUS,
when St. Vincent de Paul's plan for his life didn't turn out the way he wanted,
you guided him to discover his true calling to care for the needy.
Help us not to focus only on what we want
but also to be open to your call to serve others.
Thank you for our many blessings
and for this good food we have today.
Bless it and be with all those who are hungry, sick, or lonely this night.
Amen.

September 28: St. Lorenzo Ruiz

Lorenzo Ruiz lived a very ordinary life until he was falsely accused of murder. Lorenzo was born in Manila, Philippines, around 1600. He grew up in a Catholic family and was active in his parish church. Lorenzo and his wife, Rosario, had three children and were very happy together. But one day he was accused of murdering a Spaniard. Lorenzo knew he would not get a fair trial, so he took refuge aboard a ship with three Dominican priests. He soon learned that the ship was bound for Japan. They had planned to land in a part of Japan where people were open to Christianity, but a storm took them off course and they landed in an area very hostile to the faith. Lorenzo and his companions were arrested. For two years they were tortured horribly, but they never gave in. "Had I a thousand lives, all these to God I shall offer." St. Lorenzo is the first Filipino martyr.

DEAR GOD,
we never know the future or how our lives
might change,
but we trust you to be with us always
and to give us the strength we need to face whatever
may happen.
Thank you for the example St. Lorenzo.
Help us to imitate his trust in you and always
remain faithful.
Bless this food we share.
Amen.

September 29: Sts. Michael, Gabriel, and Raphael, Archangels

The word *angel* means "messenger of God," and the biblical stories of the angels we celebrate today all show how they performed that role. Michael appears in the book of Daniel as a great prince who defends Israel against its enemies, and in Revelation as a warrior who gains victory over the powers of evil. In the book of Tobit, Raphael is sent to help Tobit's son Tobias in his journeys. And it is Gabriel who announces to the Virgin Mary that she is to give birth to a son who would be the Messiah.

The reform of the Church's calendar joined the feasts of these three angels. Before that, today was the feast of St. Michael alone. In Europe, it was called Michaelmas, and it marked the beginning of autumn.

HOLY GOD,
your care for us is more than we can imagine,
and your love touches us in so many ways.
As once you sent your angels Michael, Gabriel,
and Raphael
to guide and protect your chosen ones,
let them be our companions, to lead and watch over us.
As we begin the new season of autumn,
may we celebrate your presence in the beauty of nature
and be messengers of your love to all those we meet.
Bless this meal we now share and bless all we do in
Jesus' name.
Amen.

October 1: St. Thérèse of Lisieux

Thérèse Martin was the youngest of five girls in her family. Her father, Louis, was a jeweler and her mother, Zélie, had a successful lace-making business. But, sadly, her mother died when Thérèse was only four. Thérèse was then cared for by her older sisters Pauline and Marie. She was very devastated when Pauline and Marie entered the Carmelite convent. She also wanted to join, but she was too young. On a pilgrimage to Rome with her father, she even dared to ask the pope to let her join before she was of age. Eventually her own bishop approved her entrance into the convent at the young age of fifteen. She is remembered for her patience with others, her desire to do little things to help them, and her ability to accept illness without complaint. She died from tuberculosis in 1897 at the age of twenty-four.

Dear God,
we thank you today for the example of St. Thérèse.
Help us to imitate her by being patient,
by going out of our way to help one another,
and by accepting difficulties without complaining.
We thank you for all the little ways your love comes to us:
in the kindness of others, in their patience with us,
and in their words of forgiveness.
We thank you for this meal and for (*name*) who prepared it.
Amen.

October 2: The Guardian Angels

Belief in guardian angels comes from the words of Jesus: "See that you do not despise one of these little ones, for I say to you that their angels in heaven always look upon the face of my Father" (Mt 18:10). Psalm 91, often a part of the Church's night prayer, also speaks of angels who watch over us: "For he commands his angels with regard to you, to guard you wherever you go" (v. 11). Our belief in angels does not mean that we will always be preserved from trouble or harm but that God's love is always with us, no matter what happens.

> LOVING GOD,
> we come together this evening to share this meal
> after a day filled with many activities.
> In our work and our play,
> in our travels and our rest,
> your presence is always with us.
> You give us the friendship of our guardian angels
> to guide us and guard us,
> to remind us of your presence,
> and to keep us on the right path.
> Help us to be aware that your love is ever near,
> and to be grateful for all the gifts that we receive
> from your generous hand, especially the gift of
> this meal.
> Amen.

October 3: St. Theodora Guérin

Providence means trusting in God's loving plan for our lives and his care for us no matter what may happen. This is what Theodora Guérin put into practice in her life. When she was fifteen, her father was attacked by bandits and murdered. Her mother fell into a deep depression and Theodora was left to care for her and her sister. When she was twenty, she wanted to join the convent, but her mother still needed her. Finally, at twenty-five, she was able to become a sister. She was soon asked to travel from France to Indiana and to begin a school. She and five other sisters faced many hardships in the wilderness, but they trusted in God's providence and were able to open many schools, orphanages, and pharmacies.

DEAR GOD,
you call each of us by name, and in your providence
you never cease to care for us.
We trust in your loving plan for our lives
and thank you for always being there when we
need you.
Please bless this meal
and give us the faith to know that we are never alone
as long as you are with us.
Amen.

October 4: St. Francis of Assisi

Francis's father was a wealthy silk merchant, and as a rich young man, Francis could do whatever he wanted. He loved to wear fine clothes and spent money recklessly. One day, while selling clothing for his father, a beggar approached him. Francis turned him away, but later regretted it and sought him out, giving him everything he had. His friends mocked him, and his father was outraged, but Francis was changing. He began to live a life devoted to prayer and simplicity. He had a vision of Jesus calling him to rebuild a rundown chapel called San Damiano. When Francis sold some of his father's wares to buy bricks for the church, his father disowned him. He traveled about, begging, preaching, and caring for the poor. Soon others joined him; they became known as Franciscans. Francis was especially aware of the beauty of all of creation and had a love for animals. He died in 1226.

O GOD, OUR CREATOR,
you have made everything—
the sun and the moon, the land and the sea,
all animals and races of people.
We thank you for all the gifts of creation
and for all that you have given us.
Help us, like Francis, to respect your world
and to use our gifts to help others.
Bless all of us, and all of your creatures
who live in our house (*you may wish to name the pets*).
And bless this meal that we share in Jesus' name.
Amen.

October 5: St. Maria Faustina Kowalska

Maria Faustina Kowalska lived a short and simple life, but her message of divine mercy has touched millions of people. Born into a poor family in Poland in 1905, she received little education and worked as a maid. When she was nineteen, she and her sister went to dance in a park. There she had a vision of Jesus suffering, and she went to a church to pray about it. She heard Jesus calling her to become a sister. She was rejected by a number of convents because of her lack of education. Once a sister, she worked as a cook, gardener, and doorkeeper. But Jesus continued to speak to her about his mercy and love for all. She wrote down these messages in her diary. He asked her to have a painting made showing how mercy flowed from his side in two rays when he was pierced by a lance as he hung on the Cross. Her diary was later published, and many copies of the painting have been made. Faustina died from tuberculosis at the age of thirty-five.

"JESUS, I TRUST IN YOU!"
Help us, Lord, to live by these words of St. Faustina
and to trust always in your mercy.
As you have forgiven us, help us to forgive one another.
May we practice patience and kindness
with our family members and others in our lives.
Bless this meal that we share
and keep us close to your merciful heart.
Amen.

October 7: Our Lady of the Rosary

The Rosary is a prayer through which we meditate on the life of Jesus and ask for Mary to pray for us and with us. An Our Father, ten Hail Marys, and the Glory Be make one decade of the Rosary. Five decades lead us to meditate on the Joyful Mysteries, five for the Sorrowful Mysteries, five for the Glorious Mysteries, and five for the Luminous Mysteries. We use a string of rosary beads to count the five decades as we pray them. The repetition of the words of these prayers is a simple way to meditate on the powerful moments that each mystery recalls. In her appearances at Lourdes and Fatima, Mary encouraged us to pray the Rosary.

> DEAR LORD, WE THANK YOU FOR THE GIFT OF THIS MEAL
> and for the loving care of your mother.
> We pray together:
> Hail Mary, full of grace,
> the Lord is with thee.
> Blessed are thou among women
> and blessed is the fruit of thy womb Jesus!
> Holy Mary, Mother of God,
> pray for us sinners,
> now and at the hour of our death.
> Amen.

October 9: St. John Henry Newman

John Henry Newman was born in London in 1801. He was the oldest of six children. His father was a banker, and John Henry received a very good education. He grew up in the Anglican Church, and in his teens he had a religious awakening and decided to become a priest. After seventeen years as an Anglican priest and teacher at Oxford University, his study and prayer led him to become a Catholic priest. He was a very influential leader and writer for the Catholic Church in England. He wrote forty books and more than twenty-one thousand of his letters still survive. He was made a saint by Pope Francis on October 13, 2019.

O GOD,
you have created me and all of us
to serve you in some special way,
in a unique way that no one else can.
This is my mission.
I may never know it in this life,
but when I am with you in the next,
I will understand it clearly.
I am a link in a chain, a special connection
between persons.
Thank you for your wonderful love for me.
Thank you for this meal we share together. Amen.

Based on a prayer by St. John Henry Newman.

October 11: St. John XXIII

Before he became pope, St. John XXIII's name was Angelo Giuseppe Roncalli. He was born in Bergamo, Italy, in 1881, the fourth of thirteen children in a poor farming family. Angelo, a bright student, was enrolled in the Franciscan seminary at the age of fourteen. He became a priest, then a bishop, and then a cardinal in Venice. In 1958, when he was almost seventy-seven years old, he was elected pope. Because of his age, no one expected him to do a lot. But he surprised the Church and the world when he called the Second Vatican Council. He said, "Throw open the windows of the Church and let the fresh air of the Spirit blow through." The council brought about many changes in the Church, including the celebration of Mass in English instead of Latin.

LORD, SEND OUT YOUR SPIRIT
and renew the face of the earth.
As you chose St. John XXIII to lead your Church
through a time of change and renewal,
give us the same joy and strength of your Holy Spirit
to accomplish whatever you call us to do,
in our family, at work and school, and with all others.
Bless this meal that we have to share
because of your goodness and love for us.
Amen.

Columbus Day

The Second Monday of October

On October 12, 1492, Columbus landed on the island of San Salvador, which is now called the Dominican Republic. Columbus had set out from Spain with three small ships: the *Niña,* the *Pínta,* and the *Santa María.* He was trying to prove that the world was round and to find a new route to India. His discovery of the New World not only proved that the world is round, but it also changed history in a way that neither the people of Europe nor the native peoples of the Americas could ever have imagined. Because Columbus was Italian, this day is especially celebrated by Italian Americans.

GOD OF ALL NATIONS,
as we celebrate this Columbus Day,
we give you thanks for our country and for all the different people
who have journeyed here from all over the world
to make it such a wonderful place.
As you gave Christopher Columbus the courage
to set sail into the unknown,
give us the courage to be open to what is new and different
in people of other races and cultures,
especially in the people we meet each day.
Bless this food that we are about to share.
Amen.

October 15: St. Teresa of Ávila

When Teresa was born in 1515, her father was a wool merchant and the richest man in Ávila, Spain. His first wife had died; Teresa was the only child of his second wife. As a child, Teresa loved to read adventure stories about knights and the saints, and when she was seven, she tried to run away with her brother to convert the Moors. Her mother died when she was eleven, and Teresa went to live in a school run by sisters. Her father and uncle wanted her to become a nun. She resisted at first, but then joined a convent known for its easy, comfortable life. But as Teresa learned more about prayer and the call of Jesus, she became more serious and devoted. She became a great teacher of prayer and wrote many books to guide people in how to pray. She led a reform of her order and suffered a lot from people who resisted this. Because of her holiness and wisdom, she was named a Doctor of the Church.

LET US PRAY THIS PRAYER OF ST. TERESA AND ASK GOD TO BLESS OUR MEAL:

Let nothing disturb you,
let nothing frighten you,
all things are passing;
God only is changeless.
Patience gains all things.
Who has God wants nothing.
God alone suffices.

Oremos esta oración de santa Teresa y pidamos que Dios bendiga nuestra cena:

Nada te turbe
nada te espante
todo se pasa
Dios no se muda.
La paciencia todo alcanza.
Quien a Dios tiene
nada le falta
Solo Dios basta.

October 18: St. Luke

Luke is the author of two books of the New Testament: the gospel named after him and the Acts of the Apostles. He traveled many times with Paul on his missionary journeys and went all the way to Rome with him. Luke was a convert from paganism and was probably also a doctor. His gospel puts special emphasis on Jesus' care for the poor, the role of women in the life of Jesus, and the importance of prayer and the Holy Spirit.

Generous God,
you gave Luke many gifts.
As a writer, a doctor, and a faithful friend,
he put those gifts to good use for the sake of others.
Help us to be aware of the many talents
we have received from you.
May we show our gratitude
by sharing them with others.
We thank you, too, for this meal.
Teach us how to share all we have received
with those in need.
We ask this in Jesus' name.
Amen.

October 19: St. Isaac Jogues, St. Jean de Brébeuf, and Companions

Isaac Jogues and Jean de Brébeuf are the best known of the eight North American martyrs. All were French Jesuits who worked in what is now New York State and the province of Quebec, Canada. They did missionary work among the Huron tribe, where they made many converts to Catholicism. They were all killed, often after prolonged torture, at the hands of the Iroquois, a rival nation that waged war upon the Hurons.

Ever-living God,
you gave St. Isaac Jogues, St. Jean de Brébeuf, and
their companions
the courage to travel to foreign lands
and to proclaim the Gospel
despite the great risks they faced.
Give us the strength to face
whatever hardships we confront
with patience and perseverance.
May the food we share at this table,
and the love we have for one another,
strengthen us to follow the path of Jesus
no matter what obstacles we meet.
We ask this in Jesus' name.
Amen.

October 22: St. John Paul II

Before he became pope, St. John Paul II's name was Karol Józef Wojtyla. As a child in Poland, he faced many hardships. His mother died of a heart attack when he was just eight. His older brother, who was a doctor, died when he caught scarlet fever from one of his patients. And when Karol was a twenty-year-old university student, his father also died of a heart attack. Karol grew up with many Jewish friends and was even the goalie on the Jewish soccer team. As a student, he was very gifted in languages—he studied thirteen different ones. He also loved acting, and he even wrote some plays. After his father died, Karol decided to become a priest. He was a seminary student when the Nazis invaded Poland and narrowly escaped capture. After the war, he served as a parish priest, university chaplain, bishop, and eventually cardinal. He was elected pope in 1978, the first time in 455 years that the pope was not an Italian. He visited 124 countries and often spoke out against injustice. One of his best-known sayings was "Be not afraid."

LORD JESUS,
throughout the many hardships and joys of St. John Paul II's life,
you gave him the courage and strength to follow you.
Teach us to "be not afraid" when we face hard times
but to rely on you for the help and guidance we need.
As we share this meal together,
we thank you for our family and for all we have.
Amen.

October 23: St. John of Capistrano

Born in Italy in 1386, John came from a prosperous family and was well educated. When he was twenty-six, he was appointed governor of the city of Perugia. But when a rival city captured Perugia, he was thrown in jail. After this, John began to think about what he should do with his life. He had a dream in which St. Francis called him to become a friar. He was ordained a priest and became a very powerful preacher and leader of the Franciscans. One of the oldest and most beautiful mission churches in California is named after him: San Juan Capistrano.

Lord Jesus,
you speak to us in many ways:
through our thoughts and feelings,
through the words of family and friends,
and sometimes even in dreams.
Help us to recognize when it is truly your voice that we hear
and then to learn how to respond to you.
Thank you for this day and all the people in it,
and for this food that we have received
through your generous love.
Amen.

October 28: Sts. Simon and Jude

Both of these apostles shared names with other apostles. Simon was also Peter's name before Jesus gave him a new name. And Jude, unfortunately, had a name very similar to Judas, who betrayed the Lord. Perhaps that's why Simon was often called "the Zealot" and Jude was known by a second name, Thaddeus. At the time of Jesus there was a group called Zealots who resisted the Roman occupation. Simon may have been a member of that group before following Jesus. Today we use the word *zealot* to describe someone who has a single-minded dedication and enthusiasm for something. Thaddeus is a name that means "courageous heart"—perhaps Jude was especially courageous. St. Jude is also known as the patron of desperate causes.

LORD JESUS,
you called Simon and Jude to be your friends
 and apostles.
You gave them the gifts of enthusiasm and courage in
 following you.
Give us those same gifts to be loving family members
and dedicated at school and at work.
Help us to believe that
even if something seems desperate or hopeless,
you are always with us.
Thank you for this meal.
May our sharing of it strengthen us and bring us
 closer together.
Amen.

October 31: Halloween

Today marks the midpoint of the season of autumn. The days between now and February 2 are the shortest days of the year. In the Celtic lands, this day was the beginning of winter. The Celts believed that on this night, demons, witches, and evil spirits roamed the earth in celebration of the season of darkness. The Celts believed you could ward off these creatures by offering them sweets, or by disguising yourself as one of them so they would leave you alone. This is the origin of our custom of wearing costumes and going trick-or-treating. We call today Halloween because it is All Hallows' (Saints) Eve.

THANK YOU, GOD, FOR THIS SPECIAL DAY,
and for the fun we have with our family, friends,
    and neighbors.
Help us to be grateful to those who are kind to us,
respectful of their property,
and generous in sharing what we receive.
Bless our trick-or-treating and all the candy we receive.
Bless this meal we now share
and keep us safe from harm.
May the light in our jack-o'-lanterns remind us of
    your love
shining through the darkness of this night.
Amen.

November 1: All Saints' Day

In the letters he wrote to the various early churches, Paul often addressed the people as "the saints." That's because all of us, as Christians, are called to be saints. A saint is a friend of God, whether in this life or the next. Today, as we celebrate All Saints' Day, we remember all those who have gone before us to enjoy eternal life with the Lord, even if they are not officially canonized. We are called to live our lives as saints on earth, following the way of Jesus. Jesus' path is especially well defined in the Beatitudes, which we hear at today's Mass.

HOLY GOD,
on this feast of All Saints we remember the words
of Jesus:
"Blessed are they who hunger and thirst
for righteousness,
for they will be satisfied."
As we gather around this table,
we thank you for this meal that satisfies our
physical needs.
We pray that you will increase our hunger and thirst
to be one with you,
so that one day we may enjoy your banquet in heaven,
together with our family and friends
who have gone before us, and with all your saints.
We ask this through Christ, our Lord.
Amen.

November 2: All Souls' Day

Praying for the dead is an ancient Christian custom. Today we pray for all those who have died because we love them and desire their eternal happiness. We ask God to bring all the departed to perfection in the joy of heaven, and we remember fondly those whom we love who have gone before us.

JESUS, GENTLE SHEPHERD,
as we gather for this meal,
we remember the many people whom we love
who are no longer with us.
Forgive all their sins
and bring them safely to your side.
As we share this food,
we trust that they, too, are seated at your
    heavenly banquet.
In your love, make us all one,
now and one day in your kingdom.
Amen.

November 2: El Día de los Muertos (The Day of the Dead)

El Día de los Muertos is a festive celebration for people of Mexican heritage. Like All Saints' Day and All Souls' Day, it is a time when we remember and pray for our family members who have died. There are actually two days: November 1 is *El Día de los Inocentes,* for remembering children who have died, and November 2 is *El Día de los Muertos,* for remembering all the dead in general. These are not sad days but days of celebration. Although they have died, our family members are still with us in a very real way. Little altars called *ofrendas* are made in the home, on which to place pictures of the dead, their favorites foods, flowers, and *calaveras,* which are sugar candies made in the shapes of skulls.

DEAR LORD, YOU ARE OUR GOOD SHEPHERD.
Today we remember our beloved family members (*say their names*).
We place them in your care,
and we pray that through your grace and in this celebration
they will always be close to us
and remain as living memories in our family.
We ask your blessing as we share this wonderful meal in memory of them.
Amen.

November 2: El Día de los Muertos

El Día de los Muertos es una celebración festiva para personas de herencia mexicana y de otros países latinoamericanos. Al igual que el Día de Todos los Santos y el Día de Todos los Fieles Difuntos, es un momento en que recordamos y rezamos por los miembros de nuestra familia que han muerto. En realidad, hay dos días: el 1 de noviembre es el Día de los Inocentes recordando a los niños que han muerto, y el 2 de noviembre es el Día de los Muertos. Estos no son días tristes, sino días de celebración. Aunque han muerto, los miembros de nuestra familia todavía están con nosotros de una manera muy real. Pequeños altares llamados *ofrendas* se hacen en el hogar. Imágenes de los muertos junto con flores, calaveras y sus comidas favoritas se colocan en las ofrendas. Las calaveras son dulces de azúcar hechos en forma de calavera. Las familias suelen visitar la tumba y comer allí.

QUERIDO SEÑOR, ERES NUESTRO BUEN PASTOR.
Hoy recordamos a nuestros queridos miembros de la familia [diga sus nombres].
Los ponemos a tu cuidado
y rezamos que por tu gracia y en esta celebración
que siempre estén cerca de nosotros
y permanezcan como un recuerdo vivo en nuestra familia.
Te pedimos bendición mientras compartimos esta maravillosa comida
en memoria de ellos.
Amén.

Election Day

The First Tuesday in November

Today citizens of the United States vote for the candidates of their choice in local, state, and national elections. Voting is both a right and a responsibility. As Catholics, we seek to inform our consciences so that we will vote for the people who best represent the values of the Gospel and the Church.

Dear God,
you have blessed our country in so many ways.
We thank you for the gifts of freedom
and ask you to help us value and protect it.
We pray today for all those who are running for office.
May they seek to lead with integrity and truthfulness
and govern with the needs of all people in mind,
especially the most vulnerable among us.
Bless this meal that we share and bless our country.
Amen.

November 9: Kristallnacht

On this night in 1938, Adolf Hitler ordered the burning and vandalizing of Jewish synagogues, schools, homes, and businesses throughout Germany. The German word *Kristallnacht*, meaning "Night of Broken Glass," refers to the broken glass all over the streets after the rioting. The police and firefighters stood by as rioters rampaged through Jewish homes and neighborhoods. It was a turning point in the persecution of the Jews in Germany. After this, Jewish children were barred from schools, curfews were imposed, and deportations to concentration camps increased dramatically.

LORD GOD,
let us never forget the hatred and violence of
the Holocaust.
Help us always to remember that small seeds of
prejudice and bigotry
can grow into acts of aggression and violence.
Remind us that the Jewish people are our brothers and
sisters in faith,
and guide us to work together for justice and peace.
Blessed are you, Lord God of all,
through your goodness we have this food to share.
May it strengthen us to pursue always charity
and justice.
Amen.

November 11: Veterans Day

Today, along with Memorial Day, is a special day for remembering those who have served in the armed forces, especially those who were killed in battle. Until 1954, this day was called Armistice Day to commemorate the signing of the peace treaty to end World War I on November 11, 1918. Now we remember all veterans on this day.

GOD OF PEACE,
we thank you for the times of peace our nation
  has enjoyed,
and we ask you to bring all wars to an end.
Today we remember all veterans,
but especially those who have been killed in wars.
We remember, too,
those who are presently serving in the armed forces.
Keep them safe
and bring them home to their families and friends.
Bless this food we share,
and give us a peace rooted in a just sharing
of the world's resources by all people.
We ask this in Jesus' name.
Amen.

November 13: St. Frances Xavier Cabrini

Frances Xavier Cabrini was born in Italy in 1850, the youngest of thirteen children. After her parents died, she sought to join the sisters who had been her teachers, but because of her poor health they did not accept her. She then worked at an orphanage. A small group of women joined her there and together they formed their own religious community. When she was twenty-seven years old, she asked the pope to send them as missionaries to China. He asked them instead to go to the United States and work with the many Italians who had immigrated there. She and six sisters came to New York where they began an orphanage and school. She also opened a number of hospitals. Mother Cabrini was the first naturalized American citizen to be made a saint.

DEAR JESUS,
thank you for the example of St. Frances Xavier Cabrini.
Although she suffered from poor health,
she did not think first about herself,
but instead dedicated herself to others.
You gave her courage to go to a new country
and to find many ways to help the poor and needy.
Help us to think not so much of ourselves but of others.
Thank you for this good food.
Bless it and bless all of us.
Amen.

November 18: St. Margaret of Scotland

St. Margaret lived almost a thousand years ago. Although she was a queen and could have enjoyed a life of ease and luxury, she devoted herself to prayer and caring for others. Every day, before she would eat, she served meals to the poor and to orphans. She would wash their feet just as Jesus had done for his disciples at the Last Supper. When she was out in public, beggars followed her everywhere, and she always had something for them. Margaret and her husband, King Malcolm, had eight children whom she lovingly cared for.

DEAR LORD,
you gave St. Margaret the grace to follow
  your teaching,
"Whatever you do for the least of my brothers
  or sisters,
you do for me."
Help us to be like her and recognize you
when we see someone hungry or homeless,
sick, suffering, or mistreated by others.
Teach us how to care for their needs
and give us hearts full of gratitude for all we have,
especially this meal.
Amen.

November 21: The Presentation of the Blessed Virgin Mary

Just as we celebrate the presentation of Jesus in the Temple on February 2, forty days after his birth on Christmas, today we celebrate the presentation of Mary in the Temple, forty days after the celebration of her birth on September 8. It was a custom among the Jews for a mother to bring her daughter or son to the Temple forty days after birth. Just as Mary and Joseph did for Jesus, so Mary's parents, Ann and Joachim, would have done for her. What we celebrate today is Mary's dedication to God and her willingness to do whatever God called her to do.

O Mary, our mother,
when the angel Gabriel appeared to you
and told you that you were to be the mother of
the Lord,
you said, "May it be done to me according to
your word,"
even though you didn't understand all that
would mean.
Pray for us, Mary, that we may have the same courage
and trust,
and help us to always be aware of all the great things
the Lord had done for us.
Amen.

November 24: St. Andrew Dung-Lac and Companions

French missionaries brought the Catholic faith to Vietnam at the beginning of the sixteenth century and it soon grew to be very strong. But many saw it as something foreign and wanted to drive it out. As a result, hundreds of thousands of Catholics were put to death by the rulers. Nevertheless, the faith of the people remained and grew even stronger. Today we remember Andrew Dung-Lac, a priest who was one of 117 martyrs canonized by Pope John Paul II in 1988. Andrew came from a poor family. When he was twelve, he and his family moved from the countryside to the city of Hanoi to find work. There he learned about Jesus and the Church and was baptized. Eventually he became a priest. He cared for and encouraged his parishioners, who lived with the fear of persecution. He was arrested three times and suffered torture before he was killed on December 21, 1835.

DEAR GOD,
we thank you for the courage and strength
of St. Andrew Dung-Lac
and all of your children who suffered and died
for their faith in Vietnam.
We pray for the Church in Vietnam today
and thank you for the many faithful Vietnamese Catholics in our country.
Help us to have the courage and strength that we need
to do what is right, even when it is hard.
Please bless this meal that we share.
Amen.

Lạy Chúa, chúng con cảm tạ Chúa đã ban sức mạnh và lòng dũng cảm cho Thánh An-rê Dũng lạc và tât cả con cái Chúa đã chịu khổ hình và chịu chêt cho niêm tin ở Viêt nam.
Hôm nay chúng con câu nguyện cho giáo hội Việt nam và tạ ơn Chúa đã ban cho quê hương Việt nam chúng con được nhiêu tín hữu nhiệt thành.
Xin ban cho chúng con sức mạnh và lòng dũng cảm để luôn làm đẹp lòng Chúa ngay cả khi gặp khó khăn, thử thách. Xin chúc lành cho bữa ăn mà chúng con sẽ chia sẽ với nhau. Amen.

Thanksgiving Day

The Fourth Thursday in November

Sometime in October of 1621, about a year after the first Pilgrims landed in New England, the first Thanksgiving celebration took place. It was a three-day feast in gratitude for the harvest, shared by the settlers of the Plymouth Colony and the Wampanoag tribe. In 1863, in the midst of the American Civil War, President Lincoln declared the last Thursday in November as a day to give thanks. In 1939, President Roosevelt made it a week earlier to allow more time for Christmas shopping. But in 1941, Congress ruled that Thanksgiving Day would be celebrated on the fourth Thursday in November. In Canada it is observed on the second Monday in October.

BOUNTIFUL GOD
you have blessed us in many ways—
in the beauty and richness of our land,
and in the freedom we enjoy.
You have given us even greater gifts
in the care of those who love us and the grace to believe in you.
May we be grateful for all these blessings,
not just today but every day.
Help us to turn our gratitude into action
by caring for those in need and working for a more just society.
Bless this wonderful meal before us,
bless each of us at this table and be with all those we love.
Amen.

November 29: Dorothy Day

Dorothy Day, who died on this date in 1980, dedicated her life to serving Christ by serving the poor. After a free-spirited youth, she converted to Catholicism and with Peter Maurin began the Catholic Worker movement. Today, Catholic Worker houses continue to shelter the homeless and feed the hungry.

God of the poor,
you gave Dorothy Day the grace
to recognize the face of Jesus
in the poor, the hungry, and the homeless.
May your Spirit guide us to recognize Jesus
in the people we meet each day.
Whether they hunger for food or for friendship,
help us to find ways to respond to their needs.
Bless this food we share.
Help us to thank you at all times,
whether in want or in plenty,
through Christ, our Lord.
Amen.

November 30: St. Andrew

One day Jesus was walking along the shore of the Sea of Galilee and he saw two brothers, Simon Peter and Andrew, fishing. He called them to follow him. They left their nets and boat and followed him right away. Andrew was one of the first apostles. He was the one who told Jesus about the boy who had five loaves and two fishes that Jesus used to feed five thousand people! Sometimes other apostles spoke to Andrew first before they went to Jesus (see Jn 12:20–22). After the Resurrection, Andrew traveled great distances to preach about Jesus, and like Jesus, he was crucified for his preaching.

LORD JESUS,
you called Andrew to be one of your closest friends
and trusted him to bring others to you.
With his brother Peter he was a brave and
faithful apostle.
Help us to hear your call,
and with our brothers and sisters
be examples of love and friendship.
As you fed the five thousand with just five loaves and
two fishes,
help us to share what we have with others.
Bless this meal.
May it nourish us as we grow closer to you.
Amen.

December 6: St. Nicholas

A fourth-century bishop from Asia Minor, St. Nicholas is the patron of children and also known as Santa Claus. Nicholas often left gifts of food or money for the poor in the dark of night, so that no one but God could see his good works. On this night, in many countries, children put shoes outside their doors to be filled with treats.

GENTLE GOD,
you gave St. Nicholas a generous heart
to care for those in need.
As we prepare for Christmas,
we remember his kindness and imitate his generosity
as we select gifts for our friends and family.
Help us to be generous,
not only to our loved ones
but to all who are in need.
Bless this meal.
May our sharing together make us ready to welcome Jesus
when he comes to us this Christmas.
Amen.

December 7: Pearl Harbor Remembrance

On this day in 1941, Japan launched a surprise attack on Pearl Harbor, the United States naval base in Honolulu, Hawaii. Some 353 planes and battleships sank or were badly damaged and 2,403 Americans were killed. This brought the United States into World War II. Between 70 and 85 million people died in the war, which finally ended in 1945 with the defeat of Germany and Japan. Today, Japan is one of the strongest allies and friends of the United States.

GOD, OUR FATHER,
you call all nations to live together in peace and justice.
Today we remember all the people who died at
Pearl Harbor
and throughout the world during World War II.
We pray for everyone serving in the military
and ask you to enlighten the minds of leaders around
the world
to work for peace and bring an end to war.
Help us to be peacemakers, too,
with our family and friends, in our schools
and neighborhoods.
Bless this food we share and give comfort to all
who suffer.
Amen.

December 8: The Immaculate Conception

This feast is not the commemoration of Jesus' conception but of Mary's. Although Joachim and Ann are not named in the Bible, an ancient tradition holds that they were Mary's parents. We believe that Mary was conceived by her parents in the natural human way, but that she was conceived without original sin. This is a gift that God gave her in anticipation of her Son's redemption. God's grace enabled Mary to live her entire life without ever sinning. Mary is revered as the patroness of the United States under this title.

O GOD,
your love is always with us,
from the first moment of our lives until the last.
As you kept Mary always close to you,
never let us stray from the way you have prepared
for us.
Make our hearts open like hers
to receive the gift of Jesus' love.
May this meal that we share
make us ready to greet him when he comes.
Bless our food, our conversation,
and the love we share in Jesus' name.
Amen.

December 9: Bl. Fulton Sheen

Today there are many preachers on television. But when television was brand-new in the 1950s, such programs didn't exist, until Bishop Fulton Sheen launched a live show called *Life Is Worth Living* in 1952. Bishop Sheen had a warm personality and a caring heart. He had previously broadcasted a Sunday-night radio program called *The Catholic Hour*, where questions and concerns of ordinary people were addressed. The audience for *Life Is Worth Living* soon grew to thirty million viewers. When he won an Emmy Award for the show he quipped, "I think it's time I paid tribute to my four writers: Matthew, Mark, Luke, and John." The program can still be seen on the Internet. Like Matthew, Mark, Luke, and John, he was a great evangelist who spread the knowledge and love of Jesus to all. Bishop Sheen died on December 9, 1979, at the age of eighty-four.

FATHER IN HEAVEN,
you gave Bl. Fulton Sheen a passion to preach the Gospel,
a loving heart, and boundless energy
to spread the Good News of Jesus in new ways to millions of people.
Help us to know and love you so much that we, too,
try to share your Good News in whatever ways we can.
We thank you for the priests and teachers who bring your Word to us,
and thank you, too, for this good food that we share.
Amen.

December 10: Thomas Merton

Thomas Merton's mother died when he was six years old. His parents were artists, and as a child Thomas lived with them in both France and New York. He went to school in England. As a teenager he said that his creed was "I believe in nothing." But as a university student he began to have an interest in Catholicism, and he read a number of books that lead to his being baptized. He felt called to become a priest, and after a retreat at a Trappist monastery in Kentucky, he entered the community there. His autobiography *The Seven Storey Mountain* and his many books about the spiritual life have inspired millions of people. Just before his death on this day in 1968, he spoke these words: "What we are asked to do is not so much to speak of Christ, but to let him live in us."

GOD OF LIGHT AND GOD OF DARKNESS,
your love is present always,
calling us to yourself in everything we do.
We thank you for the many gifts you gave
  Thomas Merton
to make him a guide for us as we seek your presence.
During this season of Advent,
give us the grace to wait patiently for your coming,
and make us alert to your Spirit's every move.
May our hunger for this meal
remind us of our hunger for you.
Bless this food and bless all who seek your face.

Amen.

December 11: St. Juan Diego

Born in 1474, Juan Diego was a simple native Mexican man. Every day he would travel from his home to the Franciscan mission for religious instruction. One day, as he was crossing a hill called Tepeyac at dawn, the Virgin Mary appeared to him. She told him to go to the bishop and ask him to build a chapel on that place. First the bishop told him to come back another day, then he asked him for a sign from the Virgin. The next day Juan needed to take care of his sick uncle, so he took a different way to avoid her. But Mary intercepted him and said, *"No estoy yo aquí, que soy tu madre?"* ("Am I not here, I who am your mother?") She told Juan to go to a hillside where only cactus grew, to collect roses there, and bring them to the bishop. Juan gathered the roses in his *tilma* (cloak). When he unfurled it to give the roses to the bishop, the image of the Virgin Mary, Our Lady of Guadalupe, was imprinted on it. Mary also appeared to his uncle and cured him.

LOVING GOD,
you choose the poor and simple ones of the world
to proclaim the Good News of your presence among us.
Just as Jesus was first revealed to the shepherds,
so, too, Mary made herself known through Juan Diego.
Make us poor in spirit and pure of heart,
so that we may be ready to welcome you.
We thank you for this food before us
and for all the gifts we receive from your goodness
through Christ, our Lord.
Amen.

December 12: Our Lady of Guadalupe

In 1531, Mary appeared to a man named Juan Diego in Tepeyac, Mexico. She told him to have the bishop build a chapel in that place. When the bishop asked him to produce proof of her appearance, he unfurled his cloak in which he was carrying roses that had miraculously bloomed in the cold of December. There on the cloak, or *tilma,* the image of the Our Lady of Guadalupe was emblazoned. This cloak with its image can still be seen today in the Basilica of Our Lady of Guadalupe in Mexico City, built upon the place of the apparition. Millions of people visit it on pilgrimage every year. Our Lady of Guadalupe is the patroness of the Americas.

O MARY, OUR LADY OF GUADALUPE,
you are here with us; you are our mother.
Lead us always to your Son, Jesus,
and by his grace give us the courage and strength
that St. Juan Diego had,
so that we, too, can be faithful disciples.
We give you thanks for this meal
and for all your blessings.
Amen.

December 12: Nuestra Señora de Guadalupe

En 1531, María se le apareció a un hombre llamado Juan Diego en Tepeyac, México. Ella le dijo que hiciera que el obispo construyera una capilla en ese lugar. Cuando el obispo le pidió que presentara pruebas de su aparición, desplegó su capa en la que llevaba rosas que habían florecido milagrosamente en el frío de diciembre. Allí, en la capa o tilma, estaba estampada la imagen de la Virgen de Guadalupe. Esta tilma con su imagen todavía se puede ver hoy en la Basílica de Nuestra Señora de Guadalupe en la Ciudad de México, construida sobre el lugar de la aparición. Millones de personas lo visitan en peregrinación cada año. Nuestra Señora de Guadalupe es la patrona de las Américas.

VIRGEN DE GUADALUPE,
venimos a darte las gracias por tenernos en tu cobijo,
por abrazarnos, amarnos y darnos tu protección todos los días.
Tu espíritu compasivo ilumina nuestro camino.
Queremos sentir tu cariño, tu compasión y tu compañía,
siempre en nuestra vida como familia.
Señor Jesús, te agradecemos por el amor de tu madre
y humildemente te pedimos que bendigas esta comida
y nos mantengas siempre bajo su cuidado.
Amén.

Esta oración está adaptada de OracionesPoderosasdeFe.com.

First Day of Winter

O GOD, OUR REFUGE,
on this first day of winter
we give you thanks for our home
and the warmth and shelter it provides for us.
During these shortest days of the year
we remember that your love is always with us,
even in times of cold and darkness.
As you sustained Mary and Joseph on their journey
to Bethlehem,
be with us as we look forward to the celebration
of Christmas.
Help us to remember all those in need of food
and shelter,
and to share with them from the many gifts you
give us.
Thank you for this meal
and for all the blessings of this joyful season.
Amen.

December 26: St. Stephen

Because St. Stephen was the first martyr (the story is told in Acts 6 and 7), he is given the honor of being remembered on the day after Christmas. Stephen was one of the original seven deacons appointed by the apostles to take care of the needs of the poor in the Church. Thus this day has been associated with taking care of the needs of the poor and the hungry, as the carol "Good King Wenceslas" reminds us.

FAITHFUL GOD,
you filled St. Stephen with the courage
to be a witness to Jesus despite his fears,
even his fear of death.
Give us the strength to be true signs of your presence,
even when, like Stephen,
we are rejected because of it.
As we share the gifts of this table,
help us to remember those who have little during
this season.
Teach us to reach out to them
with compassion and generosity.
We ask this in the name of Jesus,
our Savior and our friend.
Amen.

December 27: St. John

St. John is the second saint whose feast follows close upon Christmas. John is known as the Beloved Disciple because of the special friendship he shared with Jesus. In his first epistle John wrote, "God is love, and whoever remains in love remains in God" (1 Jn 4:16). His feast day is a good occasion to recall that of all the gifts we receive, one of the most precious is the gift of Christian love and friendship in our lives. Part of the traditional celebration of this day was the blessing and drinking of wine because, according to legend, St. John once drank a cup of poison wine without ill effect.

God of love,
you gave St. John the gift of friendship with Jesus
and revealed to him that the love we share
is truly your presence among us.
We thank you for all the ways that your love comes
to us,
especially through those who are gathered at this table.
We thank you for the food and drink we share,
and ask you to make us more mindful
of those who are hungry and thirsty.
We make this prayer through Jesus,
who is your love made visible in the world.
Amen.

December 28: Feast of the Holy Innocents

Matthew's gospel reports how King Herod, out of fear and jealousy of the newborn king, "ordered the massacre of all the boys in Bethlehem and its vicinity two years old and under" (Mt 2:16). Having been warned in a dream, Joseph took Mary and the baby and fled to Egypt. Jesus escaped, but those innocent little ones whom we remember today were the victims of Herod's insane fear.

Gracious God,
we pray for all those who suffer,
especially innocent children.
As you inspired Joseph to be the guardian of Jesus,
give us the wisdom and strength
to protect the life and well-being of children in need.
As we share this meal,
we thank you for your love,
which sustains and strengthens us
to care for others and to work for justice.
We offer this prayer in Jesus' name.
Amen.

Special Occasions

Mom's Birthday

DEAR GOD,
we thank you for Mom,
and for the love she shows us every day.
We are especially grateful for her today on her birthday:
(*each person names something about Mom that he/she is grateful for*).
Thank you for the many ways she takes good care of us,
and for her patience and understanding.
Through her love we feel your presence.
Loving God,
listen now to our prayers for Mom.
Bless her and give her good health,
and bless this meal that we share to celebrate her life.
Amen.

Dad's Birthday

DEAR GOD,
we thank you for giving us such a good dad.
As we celebrate his birthday, we thank you
for all the ways he cares for us and helps us:
(*each person names something about Dad that he/she is grateful for*).
Loving God,
we ask you to bless Dad with your strength and wisdom,
and we thank you for this meal that we share as a family.
Amen.

Child's Birthday

DEAR JESUS,
thank you for giving us (*name*) to be part of our family:
(*each person can thank God for a special quality that the birthday person possesses*).
As we celebrate his / her birthday,
we ask you to always be with him / her as a friend
and to guide him / her as he / she grows in the year ahead.
Now, dear Lord, bless this meal
that we share to celebrate (*name's*) life.
Amen.

Adult's Birthday

DEAR GOD,
as we celebrate (*name's*) birthday,
we thank you for (*name*) and for his / her love and friendship.
Thank you for (*name's*) many wonderful qualities:
(*each person can mention something he/she is grateful for*).
Thank you, Lord, for this opportunity to be together.
Bless (*name*) and keep him / her always in your care.

Grandmother's Birthday

O GOD OF LOVE,
we are so grateful for Grandma (*or whatever name the family may use*).
Thank you for giving her to us
and for all the ways she shows how much she loves us.

Watch over her in the year ahead
and keep her always in your care.
Help us to show her our love and gratitude in all the ways we can.
Bless this meal and bless everyone in our family.
Amen.

Grandfather's Birthday

O God of love,
we are so grateful for Grandpa (*or whatever name the family may use*).
Thank you for giving him to us
and for all the ways he shows how much he loves us.
Watch over him in the year ahead
and keep him always in your care.
Help us to show him our love and gratitude in all the ways we can.
Bless this meal and bless everyone in our family.
Amen.

Las Mañanitas

This is a traditional Mexican birthday song, sometimes sung to awaken a child. It is also sung on the Feast of Our Lady of Guadalupe in her honor.

Estas son las mañanitas
que cantaba el rey David.
Hoy por ser día de tu santo,
te las cantamos así.

Despierta, mi bien, despierta,
mira que ya amaneció,
ya los pajarillos cantan,
la luna ya se metió.

Qué linda está la mañana
en que vengo a saludarte,
venimos todos con gusto
y placer a felicitarte.

El día en que tu naciste,
nacieron todas las flores,
y en la pila del bautismo,
cantaron los ruiseñores.

Ya viene amaneciendo,
ya la luz del día nos dio.
Levántate de mañana,
mira que ya amaneció.

Las Mañanitas

THIS IS THE MORNING SONG
that King David sang.
Because today is your saint's day,
we're singing it for you.

Wake up, my dear, wake up,
look it is already dawn.
The birds are already singing
and the moon has set.

How lovely is the morning
in which I come to greet you.
We all came here with joy
and pleasure to congratulate you.

The day you were born
all the flowers were born.
On the baptismal font
the nightingales sang.

The morning is coming now,
the sun is giving us its light
Get up in the morning,
look it is already dawn

Baptism

FATHER,
we thank you so much for giving us (*child's name*)
to be a part of our family,
and for his/her baptism that we have just celebrated.
(*Name*) is your precious child,
united today with Christ and as a member of his Body,
the Church.
May your Holy Spirit, that (*name*) has received this day,
guide him/her always and keep him/her close to you.
Thank you for the gift of our baptisms
and for this meal that we share in celebration.
Amen.

Anniversary of a Baptism

Place the child's baptismal candle and a photo from the baptism on the table.

GOD, OUR CREATOR,
thank you for the gift of (*name*)
and for the life of Jesus that lives within him/her.

Today we remember his / her baptism,
how through water and the Holy Spirit
he / she became your child
and a member of your family, the Church.
Help (*name*) to continue to grow in your love.
Bring him / her closer to you each day
so he / she can make your light shine forth for all of us.
Bless this food that we share
in the name of Jesus, our friend and brother.
Amen.

First Communion

ALL LOVING GOD,
you created (*name*) in your image
and gave him / her the gift of life in our family.
Through Baptism you welcomed (*name*) into your family, the Church,
and called him / her to live as your son / daughter.
We thank you for this day on which, for the first time,
(*name*) received your Son, Jesus, in the Eucharist.
May we always be nourished by your presence
so as to grow in friendship with you.
As we continue our celebration around this table,
bless our food and help us to recognize Christ in one another.
We ask this in Jesus' name.
Amen.

Confirmation

God, our Creator,
from the beginning of time
your Spirit has been at work in the world,
creating, renewing, transforming all things.
We thank you today for the gift of your Spirit
whom (*name*) has received in the Sacrament
of Confirmation.
May the Holy Spirit continue to help (*name*)
to grow strong in faith and in love,
and guide him/her in all the difficult decisions
he/she will make in the future.
Bless this meal, and through our sharing of it,
renew us all with the Spirit's many gifts.
We ask this through Christ, our Lord.
Amen.

Wedding Anniversary

To be read by one of the children.

God of love,
thank you for this day
when we celebrate Mom and Dad's
wedding anniversary.
You brought them together,
and from their love our family has grown.
We thank you for their love
and ask you to give them the help that they need
to love each other even more.
Help us to remember their needs, too,
and not just think of our own.

Bless this food
and strengthen us as a family
as we share it together.
We ask this in Jesus' name.
Amen.

First Day of School

O GOD, TODAY WE BEGIN A NEW YEAR OF SCHOOL.
We thank you for all the fun we had this summer
and we ask you to be with us in the days ahead.
Send your Holy Spirit upon us
to fill us with enthusiasm for learning
and to calm our fears.
Bless our friends, old and new,
and especially our teacher(s): (*names*).
Bless this food before us.
May it strengthen our hearts and minds
to grow in your love.
We ask this in Jesus' name.
Amen.

Last Day of School

DEAR LORD,
as we come to the end of this school year,
we thank you for everything that has been a part of it:
for all we have learned, for the friends we have made,
and for our teachers and the many other people
who helped us in school.
We thank you for the happy times when we did well,
and we thank you for being with us
during the hard times when we struggled.

Bless this food that we share together,
and bless the days of summer vacation that are ahead.
We pray this in Jesus' name.
Amen.

Graduation from Elementary School

LORD JESUS,
today we give you thanks and praise
for (*name's*) graduation from (*name of school*).
You have been with him/her
through these years of growth and learning,
and your Holy Spirit has helped him/her
to reach this important milestone.
Thank you for the many gifts and talents
you have given (*name*).
Continue to guide and strengthen (*name*)
as he/she begins high school.
Bless the many teachers and school workers
who have helped him/her in the past
and those who will guide him/her in the future.
And bless this wonderful food that we share
in celebration.
Amen.

Graduation from High School

LORD JESUS,
thank you for the many ways your friendship has
guided (*name*)
through these last four years of high school.
We thank you for his/her teachers
and all those who have supported him/her.

Now as this next phase of (*name's*) life begins,
we pray that he / she may continue to grow
into maturity.
May his / her many good qualities and talents
develop and bear fruit in a life of love for family
and friends
and service to those in need.
Bless this food that we share in celebration
and keep us always close to one another and to you.
Amen.

When Friends Visit

Lord Jesus,
as we gather together for this meal,
we remember your words to your first disciples:
"I have call you friends."
We remember the many meals you shared with
your friends—
sometimes wonderful banquets,
sometimes simple meals eaten outdoors.
Be with us now as we share this meal in your name.
May our sharing of this food and drink deepen
our friendship
and help us to appreciate your presence in one another.
We ask this with trust in your love.
Amen.

When Cousins Visit

To be read by one of the children.

Dear Jesus,
we remember how much you loved your family
and especially your cousin John the Baptist.
We thank you today for the presence our
cousin(s) (*name/s*).
Be with us as we share this meal
and always keep us close to one another.
Help us especially to remember those who are hungry
or lonely
and teach us how to reach out to them.
Amen.

When Grandparents Visit

Dear God,
thank you for this time we share with
(*say whatever name you usually use for your grandparents*).
Their (his / her) love
reminds us in a special way of your love for us.
As we share this meal together,
help us to grow in love as a family.
May we always be grateful for one another
and draw strength from our love.
We give you thanks for this food
and the nourishment it provides
through Jesus, our Lord.
Amen.

To Celebrate a Special Achievement

Use this prayer to give thanks for a special accomplishment of a family member—for example, a good report card, participation in an athletic or artistic event, a new job, a raise, or an award of some kind.

DEAR GOD,
we are especially grateful tonight
for (*say what the special achievement is*).
We thank you for the many gifts you have given
to (*name*)
that have helped him/her to accomplish this.
As we share this meal in celebration,
help us to remember all the gifts
you have given to each of us.
Help us to use our gifts for others,
especially those in need.
Bless this food
and continue to bless (*name*) with your love.
Amen.

When Someone Dies

MERCIFUL FATHER,
we come to you in sadness today
as we remember (*name*).
We know that even though his/her body has died
and his/her life on earth has ended,
he/she is alive with you.
Bring (*name*) into the fullness of your love.
Help us to treasure his/her memory

and imitate his/her many good qualities.
Please bless this meal that we share in (*name's*) memory
and give us your comfort and peace.
Amen.

Anniversary of a Death

JESUS, GENTLE SHEPHERD,
we thank you for (*name*) who died
one (*or the appropriate number*) year(s) ago today.
We remember his/her love and kindness
and so many things about him/her:
(*here each person can recall a special memory*).
Good Shepherd, we trust that you have led (*name*)
through the darkness of death
to the joy of your presence.
Keep all our loved ones, living or dead,
close by your side,
and keep us close to one another.
Bless this meal and bless us with your peace.
Amen.

When a Bad Thing Happens

Use when family members want to pray about something bad that has occurred and that they are concerned about.

FATHER OF MERCY AND JUSTICE,
we come to you today with sorrow in our hearts
because of (*say what has happened*).
We have so many bad feelings
and we don't know what we can do,

but we trust in you
and your care for those who have died or been injured.
Be with those who are grieving
and give your strength to those who are responding.
We pray for peace and cooperation
and ask you to show us how we might help.
Please bless this meal and help us
to be signs of your love and forgiveness.
Amen.

When We've Had a Bad Day

This prayer can be used when there has been arguing or fighting going on.

Dear Jesus,
sometimes when we are angry
or our feelings are hurt
or things don't seem fair,
we can react in ways that hurt others
by what we say or what we do.
Help us to be calm and patient
and not to respond with anger.
We are sorry for hurting others.
Help us to forgive anyone who has hurt us.
Bless this meal and help us to live together
more peacefully.
Amen.

Traditional Graces

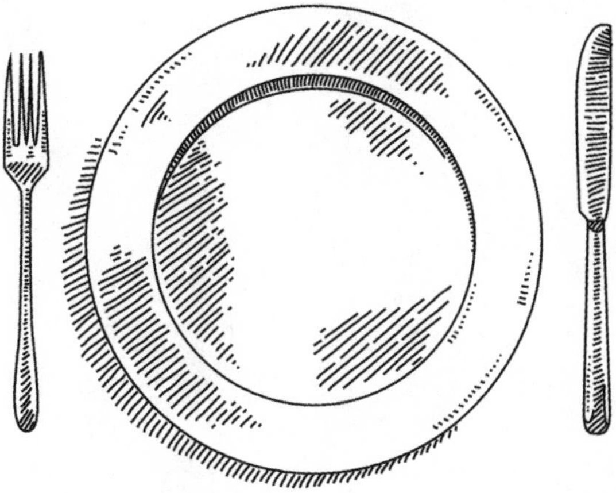

BLESS US, O LORD, AND THESE YOUR GIFTS
which we are about to receive
from your bounty through Christ our Lord. Amen.

GOD IS GREAT AND GOD IS GOOD,
and we thank God for this food.
By God's hand must all be fed;
give us, Lord, our daily bread.

BLESS, O LORD, THIS FOOD TO OUR USE,
and us to your loving service.
Make us ever mindful to the needs of others
in the name of Jesus Christ. Amen.

BLESSED ARE YOU, LORD, OUR GOD,
Creator of the universe!
Through your Word all things were made,
and by your goodness we have this food to share.
Blessed be God forever.

—Based on the Jewish blessing prayer, the Berakhah

FATHER, WE THANK THEE WHO HAST PLANTED
thy holy Name within our hearts.
Knowledge and faith and life immortal
Jesus thy Son to us imparts.

AS GRAIN, ONCE SCATTERED ON THE HILLSIDES,
was in this broken bread made one,
so from all lands thy church be gathered
into thy kingdom by thy Son.

—From the *Didache*

THE EYES OF ALL WAIT UPON YOU, O LORD,
and you give them their food in due season.
You open your hand
and fill every living thing with your blessing.

WE THANK YOU, O LORD, FOR THESE
your gifts,
and ask you to grant
that whether we eat or drink, or whatever we do,
we do it for your glory.

—The *Roman Ritual,* based on Psalm 104:27–28
and 1 Corinthians 10:31

GIVE FOOD TO THE HUNGRY, O LORD,
and hunger for you to those who have food.

BE PRESENT AT OUR TABLE, LORD,
be here and everywhere adored.
Thy creatures bless, and grant that we
may feast in paradise with thee.

—John Wesley

WE BEING MANY ARE ONE BREAD AND ONE BODY;
for we are all partakers of that one bread.
Whether therefore you eat, or drink,
or whatever you do, do all to the glory of God.

—Based on 1 Corinthians 10:17, 31

GIVE US GRATEFUL HEARTS, OUR FATHER,
for all your mercies,
and make us mindful of the needs of others.

—*Book of Common Prayer*

FOR EACH NEW MORNING WITH ITS LIGHT . . .
for rest and shelter of the night,
for health and food, for love and friends,
for everything Thy goodness sends.

—Ralph Waldo Emerson

NOW THANK WE ALL OUR GOD,
with heart and hand and voices
who wondrous things hath done,
in whom his world rejoices.

—Catherine Winkworth

THANK YOU, GOD, FOR FOOD SO GOOD.
Lord, help us do the things we should.

GOD IN ME AND GOD IN YOU,
there lies all the good we do.
We thank you, Lord, that this is so,
we thank you that we live and grow.

BENDÍCENOS, SEÑOR, A NOSOTROS.
Bendice estos alimentos que vamos a tomar.
para mantenernos en tu santo servicio.
Bendice a quienes los nos han preparado.
Dales pan a los que tienen hambre,
y hambre y sed de justicia a los que tenemos pan.
Te lo pedimos por Cristo nuestro Señor. Amén.

—Traditional Spanish grace

BENDIGAMOS AL SEÑOR, QUE NOS UNE EN CARIDAD
y nos nutre con su amor, en el pan de la unidad,
oh Padre nuestro.

—Traditional Spanish hymn

Index

D

E

F

G

H

I

J

K

L

M

N

O

P

Q

R

S

Z

Robert M. Hamma is the author of nine books and numerous articles on spirituality and family life. He retired in 2016 as vice president and editorial director at Ave Maria Press. Hamma earned a master's degree in theology from the University of Notre Dame and a master of divinity degree from Immaculate Conception Seminary. He previously worked in parish ministry and as an editor at Paulist Press. He and his wife, Kathryn Schneider, have three grown children and live in Granger, Indiana.

AVE

AVE MARIA PRESS

Founded in 1865, Ave Maria Press,
a ministry of the Congregation of
Holy Cross, is a Catholic publishing
company that serves the spiritual and
formative needs of the Church and its
schools, institutions, and ministers;
Christian individuals and families; and
others seeking spiritual nourishment.

For a complete listing of titles from

Ave Maria Press

Sorin Books

Forest of Peace

Christian Classics

visit www.avemariapress.com